LIFE AND HEALTH INSURANCE

4TH EDITION

Questions & Answers

DEARBORN™
A **Kaplan Professional** Company

This publication is designed to provide accurate and authoritative information in regard to the subject matter covered. It is sold with the understanding that the publisher is not engaged in rendering legal, accounting or other professional service. If legal advice or other expert assistance is required, the services of a competent professional person should be sought.

This text is updated periodically to reflect changes in laws and regulations. To verify that you have the most recent edition, you may call DEARBORN at 1-800-423-4723.

First printing, November 2000

ISBN: 0-7931-4506-6

INTRODUCTION

For nine years, *PASSTRAK® Life and Health Insurance Questions & Answers* has helped candidates successfully prepare for state insurance licensing examinations. Research has proven that the best way to prepare for an objective exam is to take similar practice exams. In so doing, the student can discover weak areas that may require additional study and will gain confidence in his or her test-taking ability. Because this book provides solid and efficient exam preparation, it is an indispensable final step before taking the licensing examination.

PASSTRAK® Life and Health Insurance Questions & Answers contains more than 600 multiple-choice questions in three parts: Principles of Life and Health Insurance, Principles of Life Insurance and Principles of Health Insurance. This allows the student to concentrate on life insurance or health insurance or both, depending on the exam he or she plans to take. The style, scope and format of the questions contained in this book are distinctly similar to the licensing exams conducted and administered by Assessment Systems, Inc. (ASI), Insurance Testing Corp. (ITC) or by your state insurance department. Each chapter opens with a list of the various concepts covered by the questions in that chapter. The questions are organized to follow the outline sequence; therefore, a student can readily identify topic or concept areas that require further study or review.

Each chapter concludes with answers and detailed rationale. The explanations are key to effective self-study and review and will also help pinpoint subject areas where the student is weak.

The emphasis of the material in this book is directed to subjects common to all life and health insurance licensing exams, regardless of the state or the testing organization. However, the student should note that this book does *not* contain questions dealing with specific state laws and regulations, as they vary from state to state.

PASSTRAK® Life and Health Insurance Questions & Answers can be used no matter what manual or class the student used to learn insurance. We wish you success in your career. Conscientious study on your part will help assure you of a good beginning. Good luck.

TABLE OF CONTENTS

I

PRINCIPLES OF LIFE AND HEALTH INSURANCE

1

BASIC PRINCIPLES OF LIFE AND HEALTH INSURANCE

Risk • Insurance and Risk Management •
Types of Insurers • Types of Producers •
Agent Responsibilities • Distribution Systems

1. With regard to insurance, risk can be defined as

   A. certainty regarding loss
   B. uncertainty regarding loss
   C. uncertainty regarding financial gain
   D. certainty regarding financial gain

2. The risk that involves the chance of both loss and gain is

   A. pure risk
   B. impure risk
   C. speculative risk
   D. whole risk

3. Which of the following statements pertaining to risk is NOT correct?

   A. Pure risk involves only the chance of loss; there is never a possibility of gain or profit.
   B. Uncertainty regarding financial loss is the definition of risk; therefore, it is characteristic of both pure and speculative risks.
   C. A stock market venture is an example of a pure risk.
   D. Only pure risks are insurable.

4. Which of the following risks is(are) insurable?

   A. Pure risks
   B. Speculative risks
   C. Whole risks
   D. All of the above

5. Self-insurance is an example of what risk treatment method?

   A. Avoidance
   B. Reduction
   C. Retention
   D. Transference

6. Treating risk by purchasing insurance is an example of

   A. avoiding risk
   B. transferring risk
   C. reducing risk
   D. retaining risk

7. All forms of insurance are alike in all of the following ways EXCEPT

   A. all are based on the law of large numbers
   B. all are implemented through a contractual agreement between the insurance owner and insurer
   C. the nature of the perils covered is the same
   D. all indemnify financial loss

8. Alcoholism is an example of a

   A. peril
   B. physical hazard
   C. moral hazard
   D. morale hazard

9. Which of the following statements best summarizes the function of insurance?

   A. It is a form of legalized gambling.
   B. It spreads financial risk over a large group so as to minimize the loss to any one individual.
   C. It protects against living too long.
   D. It spreads financial risk over a diverse group of people who are exposed to different risks.

10. The law of large numbers states that

    A. the smaller the number of risks combined into one group, the less uncertainty there will be as to the amount of loss that will be incurred
    B. the larger the number of risks combined into one group, the less uncertainty there will be as to the amount of loss that will be incurred
    C. the smaller the number of risks combined into one group, the larger the loss will be to any one individual in that group
    D. the larger the number of risks combined into one group, the smaller the loss will be to any one individual in that group

11. Assume there are four different mortality tables. Of these, the most reliable would be the mortality table covering

    A. 100,000 lives
    B. 500,000 lives
    C. 4,000,000 lives
    D. 10,000,000 lives

12. All of the following are elements of an insurable risk EXCEPT

    A. the loss must be due to chance
    B. the loss must be predictable
    C. the loss must be catastrophic
    D. the loss must have a determinable value

13. The amount of money an insurer sets away to pay future claims is called the

    A. premium
    B. reserve
    C. dividend
    D. accumulated interest

14. Which of the following constitutes an insurable interest?

    A. The policyowner must expect to benefit from the insured's death.
    B. The policyowner must expect to suffer a loss when the insured dies or becomes disabled.
    C. The beneficiary, by definition, has an insurable interest in the insured.
    D. The insured must have a personal or business relationship with the beneficiary.

15. With regard to life insurance, all of the following statements are true EXCEPT

    A. all individuals are considered to have insurable interests in themselves
    B. spouses are automatically considered to have insurable interests in each other
    C. a creditor has an insurable interest in a debtor
    D. insurable interest must be maintained throughout the life of the contract

16. In order to be insured, a group must be randomly selected in order to avoid

    A. chance of loss
    B. catastrophic loss
    C. adverse selection
    D. increase in premium

17. Suppose a life insurance company is organized in Detroit where it maintains its home office. In Michigan, the company is classified as a

    A. domestic company
    B. local company
    C. foreign company
    D. preferred company

18. Which term correctly describes a life insurance company that has been organized outside the United States or its possessions?

    A. Foreign
    B. Alien
    C. Remote
    D. Distant

19. A life insurance company organized in Pennsylvania, with its home office in Philadelphia, is licensed to conduct business in New York. In New York, this company is classified as a(n)

    A. domestic company
    B. alien company
    C. foreign company
    D. regional company

20. Which of the following statements pertaining to life insurance companies is(are) correct?

    A. If a certain life insurance company is owned by its policyholders, it is a stock company.
    B. The primary purpose of a life insurance company that is organized as a stock company is to earn a profit for its stockholders.
    C. A stock company that issues both participating and nonparticipating life insurance policies is classified as a full-lines company.
    D. All of the above statements are correct.

21. An insurance company that is owned by its policyholders is known as a

    A. stock insurance company
    B. mutual life insurance company
    C. parent company
    D. domestic company

22. All of the following statements about participating policies are true EXCEPT

    A. they are only issued by stock companies
    B. the annual premium rate is generally higher than that for nonparticipating policies
    C. they enable the policyowner to share in the earnings of the company
    D. they are eligible for dividends

23. The term mutualization refers to

    A. dissolution of an insurance company
    B. transferring control of a company from policyholders to stockholders
    C. sharing company profits with stockholders
    D. transferring control of a company from stockholders to policyowners

24. A stock company that issues both participating and nonparticipating policies is classified as a(n)

    A. all-lines company
    B. blended company
    C. mixed company
    D. combined company

25. An advance premium assessable mutual company

    A. is a stock company
    B. assesses each member for his or her portion of the losses that actually occur
    C. is owned by its stockholders
    D. charges a premium at the beginning of the policy period

26. In order to qualify as a fraternal benefit society, an organization must have

    A. a lodge system
    B. ritualistic work
    C. a representative form of government
    D. all of the above

27. All of the following may be classified as service organizations EXCEPT a

    A. health insurance company
    B. health maintenance organization
    C. Blue Cross/Blue Shield organization
    D. preferred provider organization

28. Which of the following organizations contracts with select doctors and hospitals to be a health-care provider for its members?

    A. HMO
    B. PPO
    C. DOA
    D. DPO

29. Health maintenance organizations are known for stressing

    A. preventive medicine and early treatment
    B. state-sponsored health-care plans
    C. in-hospital care and services
    D. health-care services for government employees

30. Under what system do a group of doctors and hospitals in a designated area contract with an insurer to provide services at a prearranged cost to the insured?

    A. HMO
    B. PPO
    C. DOA
    D. DPO

31. A group of individuals who agree to share each other's losses is known as a

    A. mixed group
    B. reciprocal
    C. reinsurer
    D. service organization

32. An insurer of an insurer is known as a

    A. mixed group
    B. reciprocal
    C. reinsurer
    D. service organization

33. All of the following are examples of social insurance EXCEPT

    A. Social Security
    B. Medicare
    C. Blue Cross/Blue Shield coverage
    D. workers' compensation

34. With regard to medical benefits available through the federal government, Medicaid provides

    A. medical benefits exclusively for the aged
    B. funds to states to assist their medical public assistance programs
    C. medical benefits for the disabled, regardless of income
    D. medical benefits to all who have contributed to its funding through payroll taxes

35. What kinds of benefits are available under Social Security?

    A. Death benefits
    B. Old-age benefits
    C. Disability benefits
    D. All of the above

36. Under Social Security, a currently insured worker is eligible for

    A. old-age benefits only
    B. death benefits only
    C. current benefits only
    D. old-age and disability benefits only

37. Under Social Security, a worker's primary insurance amount (PIA) is

    A. a total of benefits received during the first year of retirement
    B. an amount equal to the worker's full retirement benefit at age 65 or disability benefit
    C. the amount his or her surviving spouse will receive upon the worker's death
    D. larger than the combined insurance benefit payable to the worker and spouse at age 62

38. Lee has a Social Security PIA of $800 at the time of his death. How much is payable to his surviving spouse as a lump-sum death benefit under Social Security?

    A. $0
    B. $255
    C. $500
    D. $800

39. All of the following statements are true about service members and veterans life insurance EXCEPT

    A. the Veterans Group Life Insurance (VGLI) program offers servicemembers leaving active duty a means by which to convert their Servicemembers' Group Life Insurance policies to five-year term policies
    B. the Servicemembers' Group Life are term policies available to all active members of the military
    C. Servicemembers' Group Life and Veterans Group Life policies are issued by the government
    D. Servicemembers' Group Life insurance remains effective 120 days following discharge from the service

40. Social Security benefits are financed by a special tax paid by

    A. employers as a percentage of their profits
    B. state and local governments
    C. business, based on the amount of their assets
    D. employees, employers and those who are self-employed

41. Whether a person is fully or currently insured under the Social Security program depends upon his or her

    A. Average Indexed Monthly Earnings
    B. quarters of coverage under the system
    C. number of dependents
    D. annual salary

42. Ron is eligible for full death, retirement and disability benefits under Social Security. His work status is

    A. completely insured
    B. currently insured
    C. fully insured
    D. partially insured

43. Self-insurance is

    A. insurance written by an insurer on itself
    B. practiced by organizations that establish reserves to protect themselves against loss
    C. illegal in many states
    D. available through the federal government

44. In an insurance transaction, who does a licensed agent legally represent?

    A. Insurer
    B. Applicant/insured
    C. State insurance department
    D. All of the above

45. An individual appointed by an insurer to administer its business in a given territory is called a

    A. general agent
    B. special agent
    C. broker
    D. career agent

46. A field representative who works between the insurance company's central office and the agency force in his or her territory is a

    A. general agent
    B. special agent
    C. broker
    D. career agent

47. Which of the following statements pertaining to agents and brokers is correct?

    A. A contract of agency defines the authority of a broker.
    B. In no case may an agent be held legally responsible for actions not authorized by his or her company.
    C. Technically, a broker represents the client in an insurance transaction.
    D. A broker who places business with multiple companies needs only one broker's license.

48. In what ways does an agent represent his or her company?

    A. The agent solicits applications for insurance.
    B. The agent describes the company's policies to prospects.
    C. The agent collects premiums from applicants and policyowners.
    D. All of the above

49. Agency law encompasses all of the following EXCEPT

    A. the acts of an agent are the acts of the principal
    B. a contract completed by the agent on behalf of the principal is a contract of the principal
    C. knowledge of the principal is knowledge of the agent
    D. payments made to an agent on behalf of the principal are payments made to the principal

50. All of the following are agent responsibilities toward the applicant EXCEPT

    A. explaining the coverage
    B. delivering the policy
    C. prepaying the initial premium
    D. collecting the initial premium

51. The authority that an insurer gives to its agents by means of the agent's contract is known as

    A. express authority
    B. implied authority
    C. fiduciary responsibility
    D. general authority

52. The term for an individual who occupies a position of trust when handling the financial affairs of another is

    A. fiduciary
    B. trustee
    C. superior
    D. consultant

53. An agent in the XYZ Insurance Company, equipped with business cards, sample XYZ policies and an XYZ rate book, informs a prospect that XYZ has given him unlimited binding authority. The prospect assumes this is true. Given the prospect's assumption, which of the following correctly defines the agents authority in this case?

    A. Express authority
    B. Implied authority
    C. Apparent authority
    D. Binding authority

54. Insurers that deal directly with insureds without the use of agents are known as

    A. independent insurers
    B. direct writers
    C. mass marketers
    D. reciprocals

55. Which of the following statements regarding mass marketing insurance is(are) true?

    A. It takes advantage of small group situations.
    B. It is considered unethical and has been outlawed in some states.
    C. It involves one-on-one meetings between prospects and agents.
    D. It is marketed through various forms of print, visual and aural media.

Answers & Rationale

1. **B.** Risk refers to the uncertainty of financial loss. Insurance replaces the uncertainty of risk with guarantees.

2. **C.** Speculative risks involve the chance of both loss and gain. For example, the placement of a bet at a race track is a speculative risk.

3. **C.** A stock market venture involves the chance of both gain and loss and is, therefore, a speculative risk. Pure risk involves only the chance of loss.

4. **A.** Only pure risks are insurable since they involve the chance of loss only.

5. **C.** Self-insurance is a form of risk retention because the individual personally retains the risk and must accept the economic loss if the risk becomes a reality.

6. **B.** Purchasing insurance is the most common method of transferring risk. The burden of carrying the risk and indemnifying the financial or economic loss is transferred from the individual to the insurance company through the insurance contract.

7. **C.** The major difference between life insurance and other forms of insurance is that life insurance covers a certain risk—death—whereas the others insure against contingencies that may or may not happen—sickness, fire or theft. The only uncertainty about the risk of death is when it will take place.

8. **C.** A peril is the specific event causing loss. A hazard is any factor that gives rise to a peril. A moral hazard is a subjective characteristic of the insured that increases the chance of loss.

9. **B.** The function of insurance is to safeguard against financial loss by having the losses of a few paid by the contributions of many who are exposed to the same risk.

10. **B.** The law of large numbers operates under the principle that the larger the number of similar risks combined into one group, the less uncertainty there will be as to the amount of loss that group will incur. Thus, an insurance company is able to determine in advance the approximate number of claims it will receive in a given time period for a given risk, and place its business on a nonspeculative basis.

11. **D.** The larger the group, the more certain or reliable will be the amount of loss (which, in this case, is the death or mortality rate).

12. **C.** One of the criteria for an insurable risk is that it not be catastrophic. A principle of insurance holds that only a small portion of a given group will experience loss at any one time. Risks that would adversely affect large numbers of people or large amounts of property—wars or floods, for example—are typically not insurable.

13. **B.** Reserves can be defined as the amounts that are set aside to fulfill the insurance company's obligation to pay future claims.

14. **B.** Insurable interest requires that the policyowner be expected to benefit from the insured's continuing to live or enjoying good health or to suffer a loss when the insured dies or is disabled. An insurable interest must exist between the applicant and the insured. It does not need to exist between the applicant and the beneficiary.

15. **D.** Insurable interest is required only when a contract is issued. It does not have to be maintained throughout the life of the contract nor is it necessary at the time of a claim.

16. **C.** Adverse selection exists when an insurer has more bad risks than good, resulting in a group of policyowners whose mortality or morbidity experience exceeds the normal or expected rates.

17. **A.** An insurer is termed domestic in a state when it is incorporated in that state.

18. **B.** An alien company is one that is incorporated or organized under the laws of any foreign nation, province or territory.

19. **C.** A foreign company operates within a state in which it is not chartered and in which its home office is not located.

20. **B.**   Stock companies are owned by stockholders, not policyowners, and they are organized for the purpose of making a profit for their stockholders.

21. **B.**   A mutual life insurance company is a corporation, but there are no stockholders. Instead, the company is owned by its policyholders, from whom its resources are derived. Its assets and income are held for the benefit of the policyholders who, as contractual creditors, have the right to vote for directors or trustees.

22. **A.**   Participating policies are issued by both stock and mutual companies. They are called participating because they are eligible for dividends, thus enabling policyholders to share in the earnings of the company. For this reason, the premium cost is generally higher for participating policies than nonparticipating policies.

23. **D.**   Mutualization is the term used to describe the process whereby a stock company (one owned by stockholders) becomes a mutual company (one owned by policyholders) through the transfer of control from stockholders to policyholders. Conversely, demutualization occurs when control switches to stockholders from policyholders.

24. **C.**   Stock companies generally sell nonparticipating policies. Mutual companies generally sell participating policies. When a company sells both, it is known as a mixed company.

25. **D.**   Most mutual companies are categorized as advance premium assessable mutual companies and charge a premium in advance, at the beginning of the policy period.

26. **D.**   Noted for their benevolent and charitable activities, fraternal societies are nonprofit organizations that operate for the benefit of their memberships. To retain their tax-exempt status, fraternals must have a lodge system that includes ritualistic work and operate under a representative (elected) form of government.

27. **A.**   Service organizations offer health insurance and health care services. They do not include private insurers.

28. **A.**   A Health Maintenance Organization (HMO) contracts with select doctors and hospitals to be a health-care provider for its members. Enrollees in the HMO receive services for a fixed premium paid in advance.

29. **A.**   HMOs stress preventive medicine and early treatment, including routine physicals and doctor's calls.

30. **B.**   PPOs are groups of doctors and hospitals that contract with an insurer to provide services at a prearranged cost, thus allowing insureds to choose among these groups.

31. **B.**   A reciprocal or reciprocal exchange is an unincorporated mutual organized for the mutual protection of its members.

32. **C.**   A reinsurer insures part of the life insurance underwritten by another life insurance company to reduce the possible large loss of the latter.

33. **C.**   Social insurance is provided by the federal and state governments and includes Social Security (death, old-age and disability benefits), Medicare, Medicaid and Workers' Compensation. Blue Cross and Blue Shield are examples of service insurers.

34. **B.**   Medicaid provides funds to states to assist their medical public assistance programs. Medicare provides health benefits for the aged and disabled.

35. **D.**   Social Security provides death benefits, old-age (retirement) benefits and disability benefits to eligible workers.

36. **B.**   A currently insured worker (one who has only six quarters of coverage during the 13 calendar quarters preceding death) is only eligible for death benefits under Social Security. To be eligible for death, retirement and disability benefits, a worker must be fully insured.

37. **B.**   Primary Insurance Amount (PIA) is the amount equal to a worker's full retirement benefit at age 65 or his or her disability benefit. Benefits are reduced if a worker retires before age 65.

38. **B.**   The Social Security lump-sum death benefit is a one-time-only payment of $255 to a deceased worker's surviving spouse or eligible children.

39. **C.**   Both SGLI and VGLI are issued by private commercial insurers who participate in the programs.

40. **D.**   Employees, employers and those who are self-employed pay taxes to finance Social Security benefits. These taxes are based on the tax rate (which changes periodically) and an employees earnings.

41. **B.**   A worker's insured status determines the types of benefits the worker is entitled to receive. It depends on the number of a worker's quarters of coverage. A quarter of coverage is any three-month period commencing on the first day of January, April, June or October. Minimum quarter earnings are required and are based on national (adjusted) average wages.

42. **C.**   Fully insured is a status of complete eligibility that provides benefits for retirement, disability and death. A worker who is currently insured is not eligible for retirement benefits.

43. **B.**   Self-insurance is a legitimate method of insuring loss by establishing one's own reserve of funds.

44. **A.**   Under the law of agency, agents represent insurers.

45. **A.**   A life and health general agent is an individual appointed by an insurer to administer its business in a given territory. The individual is responsible for building his or her own agency and field force.

46. **B.**   Special agents work between a home office and the agency force. They are often called upon to resolve problems in the field.

47. **C.**   An agent represents a company while a broker represents a client. An agent may be held liable for acts beyond his or her authority if the public can reasonably assume he or she has authority for those acts. A contract of agency defines the authority of an agent. A broker is required to have a broker's contract with every company he or she does business with.

48. **D.**   An agent is authorized to solicit applications, describe the company's policies to prospects and potential clients, collect premiums and render service to both prospects and existing clients.

49. **C.**   A fundamental rule of agency law states that information known to the agent is also known by the principal, as long as the agency relationship exists.

50. **C.**   The agent has no responsibility to pay a clients premium, in advance or otherwise.

51. **A.**   Express authority is what the insurer intends to, and in fact does, give to its agent through means of the agent's contract. This authority explicitly appoints the agent to act on behalf of the insurer.

52. **A.**   A fiduciary is an individual occupying a position of trust and confidence when handling or supervising the funds or the affairs of another. A trustee is a person appointed or required by law to execute a trust to the benefit or use of another.

53. **C.**   Apparent authority is what a third party (such as a member of the public) assumes an agent has, based on the actions or words of the principal. By supplying the agent with business cards, sample policies and rate books, the insurance company has given the impression that it supports the words and actions of its agent.

54. **B.**   A large volume of insurance is sold through direct-writing companies that do not use agents, but instead employ their own salespersons.

55. **D.**   Mass marketing insurance takes advantage of large group situations, selling through direct mail, newspapers, radio and television. It is an acceptable means of marketing insurance, though there is usually little client contact with an agent or broker.

2

USES OF LIFE AND HEALTH INSURANCE

Individual Uses • Business Uses •
Estate Planning Uses •
Insurance as an Investment

1. Which of the following statements pertaining to the late Dr. S. S. Huebner's human life value concept is(are) correct?

    A. A human life value may be determined by discounting a person's future net earnings for family purposes at a reasonable rate of interest.
    B. A person's total estimated earnings at age 65, plus estimated Social Security benefits for a ten-year period, represent a human life value.
    C. A human life value is equal to the sum of an individual's current earnings.
    D. All of the above statements are correct.

2. Human life value can be expressed as a(n)

    A. economic factor
    B. priceless commodity
    C. unit of productivity
    D. dollar valuation

3. All of the following usually are included in a final expense fund when determining life insurance needs of a family EXCEPT

    A. last illness and funeral costs
    B. outstanding debts
    C. funds to pay off a mortgage
    D. unpaid federal and state taxes

4. When does a surviving family have the greatest need for income?

    A. Immediately after the death of the breadwinner
    B. While the children are growing up
    C. After the children are independent
    D. During the surviving spouses old age

5. With regard to a breadwinner's death, the blackout period generally can be defined as

    A. the period during which children are living at home and dependent
    B. the period from when the youngest child is grown to the surviving parents retirement age
    C. a time when life insurance rarely is needed
    D. the period from the surviving spouse's retirement to death

6. Which of the following terms refers to that period following the death of a breadwinner during which the children are living at home?

    A. Blackout period
    B. Child-rearing period
    C. Provision period
    D. Dependency period

7. Which of the following statements pertaining to sole proprietor buy-sell plans is correct?

   A. Concerning disposition of the business at his or her death, the only alternatives open to a sole proprietor are to dissolve the business or leave it to an heir as a bequest.
   B. A buy-sell agreement for a sole proprietor can be drafted by the proprietor or his or her life insurance agent.
   C. Life insurance is an ideal medium for funding a buy-sell agreement because, for a reasonable premium, it makes money available when needed to activate the sale of the business.
   D. In a sole proprietor buy-sell agreement, the sole proprietor is the owner of the policy.

8. Which of the following statements pertaining to partnership buy-sell plans is(are) correct?

   A. By law, a partnership ceases to exist when a partner dies.
   B. Homer and Wilbur are partners. Each buys an insurance policy to insure the life of the other; therefore, their buy-sell agreement is an entity plan.
   C. In a cross-purchase plan, the partnership is a party to the buy-sell agreement.
   D. All of the above statements are correct.

9. Three equal partners in a business worth $600,000 decide to set up an insured cross-purchase buy-sell agreement. How large a policy would each partner buy to insure the lives of the other partners?

   A. $50,000
   B. $100,000
   C. $150,000
   D. $200,000

10. Hazel, Philip and Anita are equal partners in a partnership worth $150,000. They decide to install an insured cross-purchase buy-sell agreement. Which of the following statements pertaining to this arrangement is(are) correct?

    A. Hazel will purchase and maintain a $25,000 life insurance policy each on the lives of Philip and Anita.
    B. The partnership will purchase and maintain a $50,000 policy on each of the partners lives.
    C. If Hazel dies, Philip and Anita will each have a partnership interest of $50,000.
    D. Each individual partner must purchase and maintain a $50,000 policy on each of the other partners lives.

11. With three partners in a business, how many life insurance policies would be required to insure an entity buy-sell plan?

    A. Three
    B. Six
    C. Eight
    D. Nine

12. A company with five partners is considering a buy-sell plan. All of the following statements pertaining to buy-sell plans and this partnership are correct EXCEPT

    A. if they decide on an insured entity buy-sell agreement, it would be funded with a total of five life insurance policies
    B. if they use a cross-purchase plan, each partner would have to purchase four policies, or a total of 20 policies
    C. if the company installed an entity buy-sell agreement, the business would be party to the agreement
    D. no benefits will accrue to the partnership from the buy-sell agreement until one of the partners dies

13. A company's total stock is valued at $480,000 and held in equal shares by four stockholder-employees who have finalized an insured stock-redemption agreement. How much life insurance must be purchased on the life of each of the four individuals to fund the buy-sell plan?

   A. $90,000
   B. $120,000
   C. $180,000
   D. $480,000

14. Which of the following statements pertaining to buy-sell plans in close corporations is(are) correct?

   A. A close corporation that has four stockholder-employees plans to set up an insured buy-sell agreement. A stock redemption plan will require fewer policies than a cross-purchase plan.
   B. A corporation has an insured cross-purchase buy-sell plan agreed to by the corporate president and vice president, the two owners. The president and vice president own and pay the premiums for the life insurance policies in the plan.
   C. A corporation finalizes a stock redemption agreement for its three officers, all stockholder-employees. The firms total stock is valued at $600,000 and held in equal shares by the three officers. A $200,000 policy will be purchased by the corporation on the life of each of its three officers.
   D. All of the above statements are correct.

15. Assume a dentist is insured in a business overhead expense policy that pays maximum monthly benefits of $3,000. The dentist became disabled and had covered expenses for the month totaling $1,500. Benefits payable would be

   A. $1,500
   B. $3,000
   C. $3,150
   D. $4,500

16. Which of the following statements pertaining to key-person life insurance is(are) correct?

   A. The insured key person controls the policy.
   B. The policy is a company-owned asset.
   C. At the death of the key person, proceeds are paid to his or her beneficiary.
   D. All of the above statements are correct.

17. Which of the following statements pertaining to key-person life insurance is NOT correct?

   A. A key employee is any person whose contribution to the success of a business is essential.
   B. The ABC Company insured the life of its company president for $150,000. The ABC Company is the owner of the key-executive policy.
   C. The ABC Company purchased a $75,000 permanent life insurance policy on its general sales manager five years ago. This likely was reflected each year in the company's balance sheet as a loss.
   D. The ABC Company is the beneficiary of the key-person life insurance policies on its president and general sales manager.

18. Who drafts the buy-sell agreement for a sole proprietor?

   A. An attorney-at-law
   B. A person of the proprietor's choice
   C. An insurance consultant
   D. Any of the above

19. All of the following statements pertaining to business key person health insurance are correct EXCEPT

    A. premiums are tax deductible as a business expense
    B. benefits, when paid, are treated as taxable income
    C. these policies are used to indemnify a business in the case of a merger with another company
    D. proceeds from the policy may be used to buy out the interest of a partner or stockholder who becomes totally disabled

20. Which of the following statements pertaining to key-person life insurance is(are) correct?

    A. A company insures the life of its controller with a key-employee life insurance policy. The premiums are tax deductible, but if the controller dies, the policy proceeds would be taxable.
    B. A corporation has key-executive life insurance on its president and vice president. The policies show a current total cash value of $15,500, which may be used by the corporation for emergencies.
    C. Both A and B are correct.
    D. Neither A nor B is correct.

21. At a certain point in time, an employee will have a nonforfeitable right to the money contributed to a pension plan by the employer. This right is known as a

    A. proprietary interest
    B. vested interest
    C. contributory interest
    D. possessive interest

22. All of the following statements pertaining to qualified pension plans are correct EXCEPT

    A. the employer's contributions on the employee's behalf are tax deductible to the employer
    B. the employer's contributions are limited in amount by current tax law
    C. the employer's contributions become fixed liabilities for the employer
    D. the interest on the employer's contributions is included in the employee's gross income and is currently taxable

23. Robert and his employer agree on the purchase of a split-dollar life insurance policy. If it is a traditional plan, each year the employer will contribute to the premium an amount equal to

    A. one-half of the premium
    B. the annual dividend
    C. the increase in the policy's cash value
    D. two-thirds of the premium

24. All of the following statements regarding nonqualified deferred compensation plans are correct EXCEPT

    A. a deferred compensation plan is an unsecured promise made by an employer to pay an employee part of his or her compensation in the future
    B. under a nonqualified deferred compensation plan, an employee can rely on guaranteed future benefits
    C. the employer receives no tax deduction for the amount of the compensation deferred until such amounts are actually distributed
    D. most deferred compensation plans are unfunded

25. Which of the following statements pertaining to salary continuation plans is correct?

    A. Like a deferred compensation plan, a salary continuation plan is funded by the employee.
    B. Like a deferred compensation plan, a salary continuation plan is a salary reduction-type plan.
    C. A business may set up a salary continuation plan with an independent contractor.
    D. Like a deferred compensation plan, a salary continuation plan gives the employee benefits in lieu of a current raise or bonus.

26. Which of the following would be a source of instant liquidity upon the death of an estate owner?

    A. His or her home
    B. Debts payable to the estate
    C. A life insurance policy on the estate owner's life, payable to the estate
    D. All of the above

27. In what ways could a life insurance policy be used to benefit a qualified charitable organization?

    A. The policy and its values could be assigned outright to the organization.
    B. The organization could be named as the policy's beneficiary.
    C. Both A and B
    D. Neither A nor B

28. John names the United Way as the beneficiary of his $250,000 life insurance policy. At John's death, who is responsible for the income taxes payable on the lump-sum proceeds received by the charity?

    A. John's estate
    B. The United Way
    C. The tax liability is split evenly between John's estate and the United Way.
    D. There is no income tax payable on the death proceeds.

29. All of the following are advantages of life insurance as property EXCEPT

    A. the death proceeds create an instant estate
    B. the death proceeds payable to a beneficiary are protected from the insured's creditors
    C. the death proceeds are exempt from federal estate tax
    D. the policy's value is guaranteed

Answers & Rationale

1. **A.**   The human life value concept is based on the fact that individuals who are financially responsible for the welfare of themselves and others have a monetary value. This value is equal to the sum of the individual's future earnings, discounted at a reasonable rate of interest. By this formula, insurance can be tailor-made to meet specific objectives.

2. **D.**   The economic value of a person can be determined by discounting estimated future net earnings plus interest.

3. **C.**   The final expense fund is the amount of cash required at death to pay for a deceased breadwinner's last illness and funeral costs, outstanding debts, federal and state death taxes and any other unpaid taxes, legal fees, court costs, executor's fees and the like.

4. **B.**   When a covered worker dies, a surviving spouse with small children usually will be eligible for Social Security benefits. However, Social Security cannot (nor was it designed to) meet all of the needs of the family when the breadwinner dies.

5. **B.**   The blackout period refers to that period during which no Social Security benefits are payable to a surviving spouse. This period begins when the youngest child reaches age 16 and continues until the spouse retires.

6. **D.**   The dependency period refers to that period following the death of a breadwinner during which the children are living at home. The need for family income is greatest while the children are growing up.

7. **C.**   When a sole proprietor dies, the business can come to a sudden halt unless some arrangement has been made beforehand to continue the business. A buy-sell agreement funded by a life insurance policy purchased by an employee (or other party) on the life of the proprietor will transfer the business from the owner to the other party at an agreed-upon price. The agreement must be drafted by an attorney.

8. **A.**   As partnerships are dissolved automatically by the death of a partner, it is vital that a binding buy-sell agreement be established by the partners while they are living. In an entity plan, the insurance is owned by the partnership; in a cross-purchase plan, each partner owns insurance on the lives of the other partner.

9. **B.**   Each partner's share of the $600,000 business equals $200,000. Thus, if each partner were to purchase a $100,000 policy covering the lives of the other two, the benefits payable at the death of a partner—a total of $200,000—would enable the two survivors to purchase the deceased's interest in full and retain an equal partnership basis.

10. **A.**   In a cross-purchase buy-sell agreement, the partners individually agree to purchase a proportional interest of the deceased partner. In turn, the executor of the deceased's estate is directed to sell the interest to the surviving partners. The partnership itself is not a party to the agreement.

11. **A.**   In an entity agreement, the partnership acquires and maintains a life insurance policy on the lives of each partner. In contrast, in a cross-purchase buy-sell agreement, the partners individually agree to purchase the interest of the deceased partner. The number of life policies necessary to fund the agreement can be determined by the following formula, where n equals the number of partners: $n \times (n - 1)$.

12. **D.**   A buy-sell plan offers several advantages to the partners while they all are living. Customers and employees feel comfortable about the future of the business because they know the death of a partner will not destroy the business. In addition, partners themselves have more peace of mind.

13. **B.**   The amount of insurance carried by the corporation on the lives of these stockholders is equal to each shareholders proportionate share of the purchase price, or $120,000.

14. **D.**   In a close corporation, a buy-sell plan provides multiple advantages for all concerned. It usually takes one of two forms: a cross-purchase plan in which the stockholders purchase the interest of the deceased stockholder as individuals; or

a stock redemption plan in which the corporation purchases the deceased stockholder's shares. In the case of multiple stockholders, a stock redemption plan requires fewer policies than a cross-purchase plan.

15. **A.**   Business overhead expense insurance reimburses businesses for actual overhead expenses in the event the business owner becomes disabled. In this case, the actual expenses totaled $1,500.

16. **B.**   A key person is any person in an organization whose contributions are essential to its success. With key-person insurance, the owner, premium-payer and beneficiary of the policy is the business. The purpose of the insurance is to protect the business against the economic loss incurred if the key person were to die.

17. **C.**   With key-person insurance, the business itself is the owner, premium-payer and beneficiary of the policy. As a result, the policy can be considered a company-owned asset, not a loss.

18. **A.**   It is important that the plan be drawn up as a legal document and be enforceable as such. Since only those duly licensed professionals may practice law, the agreement should be drafted by an attorney-at-law.

19. **C.**   Business health insurance is a form of key-person insurance used to indemnify a business for the loss of the services of a key employee or partner, or to buy out the interest of a partner or stockholder who has become totally disabled. As such, its cost is deductible as a business expense, and benefits payable are taxable income. It is not designed to address mergers.

20. **B.**   The death proceeds or cash values of key-person insurance are a company-controlled asset, available to the company to use for emergencies. Death proceeds from the policy are not taxable nor are premiums tax-deductible.

21. **B.**   After a specified number of years, an employee becomes 100 percent vested. That is, the employee has a nonforfeitable, ownership interest of 100 percent of the contributions made on his or her behalf.

22. **D.**   A qualified pension plan meets requirements set by the federal government in order to receive favorable tax treatment. This includes the deductibility of employer contributions, and the deferral of taxes on the amount of the contributions (and the income earned) for the employee. The employer's contributions, which are limited by law, are considered liabilities to the employer.

23. **C.**   Split-dollar insurance plans enable an employer and a select employee to share premium payments toward the purchase of insurance on the employee's life. Generally, the employer contributes to the premium each year an amount equal to the increase in the policy's cash value; the employee pays the balance. At death, the employer is entitled to receive from the proceeds an amount equal to its share of the premium payments (or the cash value, if greater); the employee's beneficiary receives the balance.

24. **B.**   Since most nonqualified deferred compensation plans are unfunded, an employee cannot rely on guaranteed future benefits. Typically, the employer finances its obligations on a pay-as-you-go basis.

25. **C.**   Salary continuation plans are established as a fringe benefit to continue an employee's salary (or a portion of it) after the employee retires or becomes disabled. The money to be paid is in addition to current salary and bonuses. Deferred compensation plans are agreements between employers and employees whereby the employee reduces his or her own income by deferring the receipt of currently due salary, bonus, commission or raise until a future date. In essence, a salary continuation plan is funded by the employer; a deferred compensation plan is funded by the employee. A salary continuation plan may be set up between an employer and employees or between a business and an independent contractor.

26. **C.**   Instant liquidity means property that is readily convertible into cash without loss, or cash itself. In this example, the only asset that would provide instant liquidity would be the life insurance policy.

27. **C.**   A life insurance policy can be gifted outright, meaning that the charitable organization

becomes the owner of the policy's value. In this case, depending on how the donor and donee have set up the gift, the donor could continue to pay the premium or the charitable organization could take over the premium payments so the policy will pay its full benefit at the donor's death. As an alternative, a charitable organization could simply be named the beneficiary of the policy's proceeds, payable upon the insured's death.

28. **D.**   Lump-sum proceeds payable upon the death of the insured are not subject to income tax, regardless of the beneficiary.

29. **C.**   Life insurance proceeds can be subject to the federal estate tax if the proceeds are paid to the insured owner's estate or if the insured owner held any incidents of ownership in the policy.

3

INSURANCE INDUSTRY REGULATIONS

Federal Regulations • State Regulations

1. What did passage of the McCarran-Ferguson Act accomplish with respect to the regulation of the insurance industry?

    A. Ensured continued state regulation of insurance
    B. Taxed insurance companies for additional federal revenue
    C. Deemed insurance a form of interstate commerce
    D. Exempted insurance from all federal government regulation and taxation

2. What is the purpose of the Fair Credit Reporting Act?

    A. It prohibits insurance companies from obtaining reports on applicants from outside investigative agencies.
    B. It gives consumers the right to question reports made about them by investigative agencies.
    C. Both A and B
    D. Neither A nor B

3. Which of the following statements pertaining to the Fair Credit Reporting Act is NOT correct?

    A. A life insurance company obtains a consumer report on Burl, an applicant, without advising him of its intended action. The company has violated the Fair Credit Reporting Act.
    B. Marjorie learns that her application for life insurance has been rejected on the basis of an unfavorable consumer report. She has a right to know what information the reporting agency has on file about her and can insist that any errors in the data be corrected.
    C. The Fair Credit Reporting Act is a state law that helps to ensure accurate reporting of information about consumers.
    D. The Fair Credit Reporting Act does not apply to insurance companies who use their own staffs to investigate an applicant for insurance.

4. Among their duties, state insurance departments are responsible for

    A. examining insurers' books and records
    B. defining and controlling the kinds of insurance contracts that may be sold
    C. investigating complaints of insureds
    D. all of the above

5. Which of the following is(are) areas of operation in which state insurance departments are engaged?

   A. Issuing rules and regulations to control the business of insurance
   B. Licensing insurers, agents and brokers
   C. Approving policy forms and rates
   D. All of the above

6. The National Association of Insurance Commissioners (NAIC) has the following objectives EXCEPT

   A. to help protect policyowners' interests
   B. to assist with the formulation and passage of federal insurance legislation
   C. to encourage uniformity in state insurance laws and regulations
   D. to promote efficiency on the part of officials who administer insurance laws and regulations

7. Which of the following statements pertaining to the NAIC is(are) correct?

   A. It is a federal agency devoted to assisting states in regulating the insurance business.
   B. It is an association of top state insurance officials that has as one of its objectives, the uniformity of state insurance laws and regulations.
   C. Both A and B
   D. Neither A nor B

8. To sell insurance legally, which of the following must have a license?

   A. An insurer
   B. An agent
   C. A broker
   D. All of the above

9. In most jurisdictions, all of the following would constitute unlawful acts of rebating EXCEPT

   A. sharing a sales commission with a policyowner
   B. sending a new policyowner on an expense-paid trip to Florida
   C. sending holiday greeting cards to policyowners
   D. reducing the initial premium payable on an insurance policy

10. Which of the following is considered rebating?

    A. Leading someone to believe that coverage exists when, in fact, it does not exist
    B. Commission splitting between agents
    C. Offering a client anything of value for purchasing insurance
    D. Persuading a client to drop an existing insurance policy to purchase another

11. All of the following statements pertaining to violations of ethical selling are correct EXCEPT

    A. in some states, both the agent and a policyowner who are found guilty of rebating would be subject to penalties
    B. rebating is unlawful largely because it is a form of discrimination
    C. if an agent is convicted in a case of twisting, it can be said that he or she is probably guilty of rebating
    D. only when it is in the best interest of the policyowner should a policy replacement be recommended

12. Assume an agent stresses the following points in a sales interview while recommending a participating 30-pay life policy to a 37-year-old prospect. Which constitutes misrepresentation?

    A. The policy's cash value will build at a faster rate than in a straight life policy.
    B. The policy will be fully paid up in 30 years.
    C. The policy endows in 30 years.
    D. Dividends are not guaranteed for the future.

13. Twisting may involve any of the following actions on the part of a life insurance agent EXCEPT

    A. misrepresenting the terms of a proposed policy to a prospect
    B. making an incomplete comparison of two different policies
    C. misrepresenting the provisions of a policyowner's existing policy to promote the sale of another policy
    D. converting a client's convertible term policy to permanent insurance

14. Misrepresentation is

    A. leading someone to believe that an insurance policy provides certain benefits when it does not do so

    B. encouraging policyowners to drop existing insurance for another similar policy

    C. offering an inducement for the purchase of insurance

    D. suggesting that a client replace term insurance with whole life

15. Borrowing 100 percent of the cash value of an existing policy in order to purchase another policy is an example of

    A. rebating
    B. misrepresentation
    C. replacement
    D. twisting

16. Which of the following statements regarding policy replacement is correct?

    A. Policy replacement is prohibited by law in all states.

    B. Twisting and replacement are synonymous terms.

    C. Even if the customer wants to replace his or her existing policy, agents can effect a policy replacement only by following the replacement regulations in their state.

    D. Premiums for replacement policies are generally lower than for the existing policies they replace.

17. Which of the following statements pertaining to an agent's handling of premium money is(are) correct?

    A. An agent must not make personal use of premium money received from policyowners.

    B. An agent violating regulations concerning handling premium money may be charged with embezzlement or mishandling funds.

    C. Both A and B are correct.

    D. Neither A nor B is correct.

18. Which of the following statements pertaining to unethical selling is(are) correct?

    A. An agent tells a prospect that future policy dividends undoubtedly will be as much or more as are being paid currently. The agent is guilty of misrepresentation.

    B. An agent asserts to an applicant that the incontestable clause in a policy simply means that the policy can never be contested. The agent is guilty of misrepresentation.

    C. An agent states to a prospect that a competing insurer is charging lower premiums because it is hurting for business. The agent is guilty of defamation.

    D. All of the above are correct statements.

19. The origin of the Unfair Trade Practices Act is

    A. federal law
    B. state law
    C. NAIC model legislation
    D. SEC directive

20. The result of the Unfair Trade Practices Act was to empower state insurance departments with all of the following authority EXCEPT

    A. investigating false financial statements
    B. issuing cease and desist orders
    C. imposing penalties
    D. licensing insurers and producers

21. Which federal governmental agency shares responsibility for the supervision of insurance marketing activities with state insurance departments?

    A. Securities and Exchange Commission
    B. Federal Trade Commission
    C. Office of Management and Budget
    D. Internal Revenue Service

Answers & Rationale

1. **A.**   The McCarran-Ferguson Act allowed the regulation of insurance to remain in the hands of the states as long as they did an effective job. States were encouraged to improve and make more uniform their regulation of the insurance industry.

2. **B.**   The Fair Credit Reporting Act is a federal law that helps ensure confidential, fair and accurate reporting of information about consumers, including applicants for insurance. It does not preclude insurance companies from obtaining outside reports; however, it allows consumers to request disclosure of information contained in their reports.

3. **C.**   The Fair Credit Reporting Act is a federal law, not a state law. As corrected, the statement is also true.

4. **D.**   State insurance departments are involved in virtually every phase of the insurance process. This includes examining insurers' books and records; defining, monitoring and controlling the kinds of contracts sold; investigating insureds' complaints; issuing rules and regulations; licensing insurers, agents and brokers; and approving policy forms and rates.

5. **D.**   State insurance departments are involved in virtually every phase of the insurance process. This includes examining insurers books and records; defining, monitoring and controlling the kinds of contracts sold; investigating insureds' complaints; issuing rules and regulations; licensing insurers, agents and brokers; and approving policy forms and rates.

6. **B.**   The NAIC is an association of state insurance commissioners, directors and superintendents. It has nothing to do with the federal government. In fact, it seeks to preserve the continued regulation of insurance by the states.

7. **B.**   The NAIC is an association of state insurance commissioners, directors and superintendents. It has nothing to do with the federal government. In fact, it seeks to preserve the continued regulation of insurance by the states.

8. **D.**   Insurers and producers (agents and brokers) selling insurance in a given state must be licensed in that state for that purpose.

9. **C.**   Rebating requires an agent to give an insured something of value, such as part of the agent's commission or a substantial gift. Sending greeting cards is a simple marketing gesture of goodwill.

10. **C.**   Rebating is offering a client anything of value for purchasing the insurance.

11. **C.**   If an agent is guilty of twisting (making incomplete or untrue comparisons to coerce a sale), he or she may not be guilty of rebating (an illegal offering of something of value, such as a return of premiums to induce a sale).

12. **C.**   Any written or oral statement that does not tell the truth about a policy is a misrepresentation. A 30-pay life policy does not endow (i.e., reach a point at which cash value equals face amount) in 30 years; it is simply paid up.

13. **D.**   Twisting involves misrepresentations and incomplete comparisons with the intention of coercing a sale. It does not involve the normal servicing of a clients account, such as converting a term policy to permanent insurance.

14. **A.**   Misrepresentation is any false or misleading statement made with respect to an insurance policy. An example of misrepresentation is leading someone to believe that an insurance policy provides certain benefits when, in fact, it does not.

15. **C.**   Replacement involves replacing one policy with the purchase of another. When replacement occurs, it must adhere to existing state regulations involving full and fair disclosure.

16. **C.**   State laws do not prevent a policyowner from replacing one insurance policy with another, as long as the transaction is handled in accordance with state laws and procedures.

17. **C.**   An agent enjoys a fiduciary role with an insured. This establishes a relationship of trust. As a result, the insured must be very careful in handling money received from the insured and the

company's premiums or be subject to harsh penalties.

18. **D.** If an agent makes any written or oral statement that does not tell the exact and full truth about a policy's terms or benefits or if he or she defames another company, the agent is guilty of misrepresentation and defamation, which violate ethical sales practices.

19. **C.** The Unfair Trade Practices Act is a piece of NAIC model legislation adopted by most states, giving state insurance departments the power to investigate and control the business practices of insurers and producers.

20. **D.** The Unfair Trade Practices Act, a piece of NAIC model legislation adopted by most states, gives insurance commissioners the power to investigate alleged improper insurance practices—such as improper finances, false financial statements, boycotts or coercion—and issue cease and desist orders and penalties if necessary.

21. **A.** In the 1950s, the Federal Trade Commission (FTC) sought to control the advertising and sales literature used by the health insurance industry. In 1958, the U.S. Supreme Court held that the McCarran-Ferguson Act disallowed such supervision by the FTC. The Securities and Exchange Commission (SEC), in conjunction with state insurance departments, regulates insurers who sell only variable annuities and variable life insurance.

4

LEGAL PRINCIPLES OF THE INSURANCE CONTRACT

Definition of a Contract • Void and Voidable Contracts •
Insurable Interest • Waiver and Estoppel • Representations and
Warranties • Concealment and Misrepresentation • Agent Liability

1. "An insurance contract is prepared by one party, the insurer, rather than by negotiation between the contracting parties." Which of the following statements explains this feature of insurance contracts?

   A. The insurance contract is an aleatory contract.
   B. The insurance contract is a conditional contract.
   C. The insurance contract is a contract of adhesion.
   D. The insurance contract is a unilateral contract.

2. For an insurance contract to be enforceable, which of the following parties must be considered competent?

   A. Applicant
   B. Insured
   C. Beneficiary
   D. All of the above

3. With regard to insurance, the term consideration means the

   A. price of the contract (such as the premium)
   B. insurer's method of evaluating the applicant for coverage
   C. screening process all agents undergo prior to licensing
   D. side-by-side policy comparison by the applicant

4. A contract is voidable when it

   A. lacks one of the basic elements of a legal contract
   B. is binding unless the party with the right to set it aside wishes to do so
   C. was never in effect
   D. cannot be enforced by either party

5. Who are the parties to a life insurance contract?

   A. Agent and the policyowner
   B. Agent, the policyowner and the beneficiary
   C. Policyowner and the beneficiary
   D. Policyowner and the insuring company

6. The applicant for insurance has more to gain if the insured continues to live than if the insured dies is the rule defining

   A. one's legal capacity to enter into an insurance contract
   B. insurable interest
   C. a legal wagering contract
   D. the aleatory nature of an insurance contract

7. Alan, age 39, is married and has one small son. He is employed as a sales manager by R.J. Links, a sole proprietorship that owes much of its success to Alan's efforts. He recently borrowed $50,000 from his brother-in-law, Pete, to finance a vacation home. Based on these facts, which of the following has(have) an insurable interest in Alan's life?

   A. His spouse
   B. His employer
   C. His brother-in-law
   D. All of the above

8. In legal terms, voluntary relinquishment of a known right is called

   A. waiver
   B. concealment
   C. warranty
   D. withdrawal

9. With a life insurance contract, which of the contracting parties makes an enforceable promise?

   A. Insurer
   B. Applicant or owner
   C. Both A and B
   D. Neither A nor B

10. Statements guaranteed to be true are called

    A. waivers
    B. estoppels
    C. warranties
    D. representations

11. All statements made by an applicant in an application for life insurance generally are considered to be

    A. warranties
    B. affirmations
    C. representations
    D. declarations

12. The intentional failure to disclose known facts on an insurance application is called

    A. concealment
    B. adhesion
    C. twisting
    D. misrepresentation

13. A false statement of fact is known as

    A. concealment
    B. adhesion
    C. aleatory
    D. misrepresentation

14. Since only the insurer prepares the insurance contract, it is called a contract of

    A. estoppel
    B. adhesion
    C. unilateral terms
    D. condition

15. The fact that an insurance contract promises to pay benefits contingent on a future uncertainty (such as death or illness) makes it what type of contract?

    A. Estoppel
    B. Adhesion
    C. Aleatory
    D. Conditional

16. Since the obligations of the insurance company hinge on certain acts of the policyowner, the beneficiary, or both, the insurance contract is termed

    A. bilateral
    B. unilateral
    C. aleatory
    D. conditional

17. Which of the following statements pertaining to a life insurance contract is(are) correct?

    A. As to a life insurance contract, "unilateral" refers to the legal obligations of the policyowner.
    B. The term "adhesion" indicates that a life insurance contract involves no exchange of equivalent values.
    C. Both A and B are correct.
    D. Neither A nor B is correct.

18. Life insurance is all of the following EXCEPT a

    A. reimbursement-type contract
    B. valued contract
    C. unilateral contract
    D. legal contract

19. With a life insurance contract, an insurable interest must exist

    A. at the inception of the contract
    B. as long as the insured lives
    C. at the insured's death
    D. at all of the above times

20. An agent's primary responsibility is to

    A. collect premiums on a regular basis
    B. act in accordance with the agency agreement
    C. submit all applications promptly
    D. renew his or her license at the appropriate time

21. In carrying out their duties, licensed insurance agents are representatives of the

    A. insureds
    B. general public
    C. insurance company
    D. state insurance department

22. An insurance agent should

    A. be honest and trustworthy
    B. be qualified to perform insurance functions
    C. have a good business reputation
    D. be/have all of the above

23. What kind of policy will protect an insurance agent against liability arising out of acts committed in his or her professional capacity?

    A. Malpractice
    B. Errors and omissions
    C. General liability
    D. Contractual liability

Answers & Rationale

1. **C.** Insurance contracts are contracts of adhesion, meaning that they are prepared by one party—the insurer. They are not negotiated contracts. In effect, the applicant adheres to the terms of the contract when he or she accepts it.

2. **A.** The applicant must be competent. The insured and beneficiary need not be considered competent if they are not the same person as the applicant.

3. **A.** Legally defined, consideration is the price requested and given for a promise or an act. In terms of insurance, it is the price of the contract, or the premium, the insured pays to keep the contract—and its promised benefits—in force.

4. **B.** A voidable contract is an agreement which, for a reason satisfactory to a court, may be set aside by one of the parties to the contract. Unless and until the contract is disaffirmed by one of its parties, however, it remains enforceable.

5. **D.** The parties to a life insurance contract are the policyowner (who was also the applicant) and the insuring company. Neither the beneficiary nor the agent are contracting parties.

6. **B.** A person acquiring a life insurance contract must be subject to loss upon the death of the individual to be insured. This is known as insurable interest and it is required before a life insurance policy will be issued.

7. **D.** Generally, a person has an insurable interest in another if they are related by blood or marriage or if their relationship is such that the insured's continuing to live will benefit that individual or the insured's death will cause that individual financial or economic loss. Spouses are assumed to have an automatic insurable interest in each other. Thus, in this case, all three individuals have an insurable interest in Alan's life.

8. **A.** A waiver is a voluntary relinquishment of a known right. If an insurer waives a legal right under an insurance policy, it cannot deny a future claim based on a violation of that right. This is known as estoppel, and the insurer is estopped from denying the claim.

9. **A.** A life insurance contract is unilateral in that only one party—the insurer—makes an enforceable promise (the promise to pay the policy's benefit if certain occurrences come to pass or certain conditions are met). The applicant or owner makes no enforceable promise and is not legally required to maintain the contract.

10. **C.** Warranties are statements guaranteed to be true. Representations are statements believed to be true.

11. **C.** Most states have passed statutes specifying that, except in instances of fraud, all statements made by an applicant when applying for insurance are considered to be representations.

12. **A.** If the applicant intentionally fails to disclose known facts that could influence the issuance of the policy (concealment), the insurer may have the grounds for voiding the policy.

13. **D.** False statements of facts, known as misrepresentations, may provide grounds for voiding the policy, even if unintentional.

14. **B.** Insurance contracts are contracts of adhesion, meaning that they are prepared by one party—the insurer. They are not negotiated contracts. In effect, the applicant adheres to the terms of the contract when he or she accepts it.

15. **C.** Insurance is an aleatory contract in that the benefit it pays is contingent upon the occurrence of a future uncertain event, such as illness or death. An aleatory contract is defined as a mutual agreement in which the effects, in respect to both losses and advantages, depend on an uncertain event.

16. **D.** Insurance is a conditional contract because the obligations of the insurance company hinge on the performance of certain acts by the insured and the beneficiary, such as the payment of premiums and furnishing proof of loss.

17. **D.** A unilateral contract in insurance refers to the insurer's legal obligations. Adhesion indicates that the contract was drafted by one party (the insurer) and must be accepted or rejected by a second party (the applicant), who cannot bargain with respect to its terms.

18.　**A.**　Life insurance is a valued contract in that it pays a stated amount. Health insurance is a reimbursement contract, reimbursing the insured for the amount of loss.

19.　**A.**　With life insurance, an insurable interest is only required upon policy application and inception. It does not have to continue through the duration of the contract, nor does it have to exist at the insured's death in order to claim the policy's proceeds. This is in contrast to property and casualty insurance, which requires that an insurable interest exist at the time of the claim.

20.　**B.**　The agency agreement is the agent's contract with the insurance company. It defines the conditions under which the agent agrees to represent the company and governs the agent's activities on behalf of the company.

21.　**C.**　An agent is a person or corporation authorized by an insurer to solicit business and collect money on behalf of the insurer.

22.　**D.**　An insurance agent must be honest, trustworthy, qualified and have a good business reputation.

23.　**B.**　Under errors and omissions insurance, the insurer agrees to pay for claims arising out of the errors and omissions of the insured agent. It is a professional liability policy.

II

Principles of Life Insurance

5

TYPES OF LIFE INSURANCE POLICIES AND RIDERS

Term • Permanent • Interest-Sensitive •
Riders • Options •
Industrial Life • Group Life

1. Jason is the insured in a $100,000, ten-year renewable term policy. Soon after taking out the policy, he develops a serious heart condition and becomes uninsurable. Which of the following statements pertaining to Jason's rights to renew this policy is correct?

   A. Since the condition manifested after the policy was issued, he will not be able to renew his policy.
   B. Jason will be able to renew the policy.
   C. It will be necessary for Jason to show evidence of insurability in order to renew the policy.
   D. If Jason renews his policy, it will be rated for his health condition.

2. A one-year renewable term policy

   A. increases in premium each year, based on the insured's health
   B. has a premium that remains the same, no matter how many times it is renewed
   C. renews with an increase in premium, based on the insured's age
   D. may not be renewed more than once

3. David has a $30,000 nonrenewable five-year term policy. The premium he pays for this policy would be

   A. more than for a $30,000, five-year renewable term policy
   B. the same as for a $30,000, five-year renewable term policy
   C. less than for a $30,000, five-year renewable term policy
   D. increased each year during the five-year period

4. Madge took out a $15,000, ten-year convertible term policy at age 30, and at age 36 decides to convert the policy to permanent insurance of the same amount on an original-age basis. All of the following statements pertaining to this situation are correct EXCEPT

   A. conversion will be contingent upon her evidence of insurability
   B. the new policy will build cash values at a faster rate than if she converts at her attained age
   C. a higher premium will be charged for the new policy
   D. she must make up the difference in premiums for the period between her ages 30 and 36

5. Which of the following statements pertaining to term insurance is(are) correct?

    A. A term policy cannot be both renewable and convertible.
    B. Janice and Ruth are the same age and have term policies of identical face amounts. Janice's policy is renewable; Ruth's policy is nonrenewable. Ruth pays the higher premium.
    C. Both A and B are correct.
    D. Neither A nor B is correct.

6. Which of the following life insurance policies having the same face value would have the highest premium if issued to the same person?

    A. Ten-year renewable level term
    B. Ten-year renewable and convertible level term
    C. Ten-year decreasing term
    D. Ten-year nonrenewable level term

7. Gerald, a 40-year-old building contractor, wants financial protection for his family while $150,000 of his assets are tied up in a building project for about five years. Which of the following types of life insurance policies would give him that protection at the lowest cost?

    A. Straight whole life
    B. Life paid-up at 45
    C. Five-year level term
    D. Single-premium whole life

8. Avis has a term insurance policy in which the amount of protection remains constant during the term period. Which kind of term insurance does Avis have?

    A. Family term
    B. Increasing term
    C. Decreasing term
    D. Level term

9. Peggy takes out a $50,000 ten-year policy on herself and names her two children, ages 11 and 12, as primary beneficiaries to share equally in the proceeds. How much would each child receive if Peggy should die when the children are ages 19 and 20, respectively?

    A. Nothing
    B. $25,000
    C. $50,000
    D. $50,000 plus the cash value in the policy

10. Frank is the insured in a $40,000, five-year level term policy issued in 1987. He died in 1993. His beneficiary received

    A. the cash value of the policy
    B. $20,000
    C. $40,000
    D. nothing

11. Chester, age 25, has a $25,000, 15-year level term policy. Joel has a $25,000, 15-year decreasing term contract. The policies were issued by the same company to the respective insureds on September 1, 1975. Which of the following statements pertaining to this situation is correct?

    A. Chester and Joel had the same amount of protection during the 15-year periods of their policies.
    B. If both insureds had died in 1988, Chester's beneficiary would have received more than Joel's beneficiary.
    C. Chester and Joel pay the same amount of premium.
    D. If both insureds had died in 1992, Chester's beneficiary would have received less than Joel's beneficiary.

12. Decreasing term insurance could be recommended for all of the following EXCEPT

    A. to protect a family while children are growing up
    B. for mortgage protection
    C. for protection while a business loan is outstanding
    D. to build a retirement fund

13. Roland is 45 years old and married. He has a son who is age 19 and a freshman at a local university. He also has a daughter, age eight. A decreasing term policy could be recommended for Roland for which of the following reasons?

    A. To supplement Roland's retirement income
    B. To guarantee that his son's college tuition will be covered
    C. To provide (an emergency) source for loans
    D. To provide a future college education for the daughter

14. Increasing term insurance is almost always sold as a(n)

    A. option
    B. rider
    C. endorsement
    D. whole life policy

15. In most states, credit life insurance is sold in the form of

    A. whole life
    B. increasing term
    C. decreasing term
    D. level term

16. The party to whom the life insurance policy cash values belong is the

    A. policyowner
    B. insured
    C. insurer
    D. beneficiary

17. How can the cash value accumulation in a straight whole life insurance policy be accessed while the insured is living and while keeping the coverage in force?

    A. Through a policy loan
    B. Through a cash value surrender
    C. Through a partial cash value withdrawal
    D. All of the above

18. A life insurance policy in which the face amount remains level and the cash value grows to an amount equal to the face amount when the insured reaches age 100 is a

    A. whole life policy
    B. term policy
    C. endowment policy
    D. limited pay life policy

19. All of the following statements pertaining to a whole life policy are correct EXCEPT

    A. the policy offers insurance protection to age 100
    B. it provides both insurance protection and living values
    C. it is designed to mature or endow at the insured's age 100
    D. the face amount may be paid as a lump sum at the policyowners selected retirement age

20. All of the following are distinguishing characteristics of straight whole life policies EXCEPT

    A. insurance protection to age 100
    B. cash values
    C. level premiums
    D. option to renew

21. Darlene owned a $30,000 whole life policy that had a $21,000 cash value when she died at the age of 75. The amount paid by the insurance company as a death benefit was

    A. nothing
    B. $21,000
    C. $30,000
    D. $51,000

22. Which of the following policies endow at age 100?

    A. Level term and whole life
    B. Whole life and limited pay life
    C. Endowment and decreasing term
    D. All endowment policies

23. Tom has a $50,000 whole life policy. If he continued to pay the required premiums and lived to age 100, he would receive

    A. nothing, as he outlived the term of the contract
    B. $50,000 as an endowment
    C. the cash surrender value, a sum less than $50,000
    D. double the face amount, or $100,000

24. Which of the following statements pertaining to limited pay life policies is(are) correct?

    A. The total premium cost for a single premium life policy is more than the total premium cost for a policy with premiums spread over a period of years.
    B. Both limited pay life and whole life policies endow at age 100.
    C. Both A and B are correct.
    D. Neither A nor B is correct.

25. Which of the following $50,000 limited pay life policies will have the highest premium for an applicant who is age 30?

    A. 20-pay life policy
    B. 25-pay life policy
    C. 30-pay life policy
    D. Life paid-up at age 65

26. All of the following statements regarding basic forms of whole life insurance are correct EXCEPT

    A. generally, straight life premiums are payable, at least annually, for the duration of the insured's life
    B. the owner of a 30-pay life policy will owe no more premiums after the thirtieth year the policy is in force
    C. limited payment life provides protection only for the years during which premiums are sold
    D. a single-premium life policy is purchased with a large one-time only premium

27. Alan is the insured in a $20,000 endowment at age 60 policy he purchased in 1979 at the age of 40. How long must he pay premiums before the policy endows?

    A. 20 years
    B. 40 years
    C. 60 years
    D. 100 years

28. At age 35, Bret bought a $25,000 life insurance policy for which the beneficiary will be paid the face amount if Bret dies before age 60. Bret is to pay the premiums until he reaches age 55, but the insurance protection continues to maturity. Which type of policy did Bret purchase?

    A. 20-pay endowment at age 60
    B. 20-pay life
    C. 30-year endowment
    D. Life paid-up at 65

29. How long does the insurance protection (amount at risk) extend in a 30-year endowment policy?

    A. To the insured's age 100
    B. One hundred years
    C. To the insured's age 65
    D. Thirty years

30. Which term would identify a policy in which the premium payments are completed in 20 years, and the policy endows when the insured turns age 60?

    A. Endowment at age 60 policy
    B. 20-pay life policy
    C. Whole life policy
    D. 20-pay endowment at age 60 policy

31. All of the following statements pertaining to a modified whole life policy are correct EXCEPT

    A. cash value builds so long as the policy is in force up to the insured's age 100
    B. premiums are uniformly lower during the early years of the contract
    C. it is basically an endowment policy
    D. the premium-paying period continues to age 100

32. Helen has just taken out a modified whole life policy. Which of the following statements pertaining to her policy is correct?

    A. The premium will be higher during the next few years and then remain constant at a lower level.
    B. The premium will be lower during the next few years and then be increased to a higher constant level.
    C. The face amount will be higher during the next few years and then remain constant at a lower level.
    D. The face amount will be lower during the next few years and then be increased to a higher constant level.

33. Gene, age 20, purchased a $35,000 life insurance policy. The premium at issue is lower than normal whole life rates, and increases each year for the first five years of the policy period. After that, the premium levels off. What type of policy does Gene own?

    A. Modified whole life
    B. Minimum deposit whole life
    C. Graded premium whole life
    D. Limited pay at age 20 whole life

34. All of the following statements pertaining to modified whole life and graded premium whole life policies are correct EXCEPT

    A. the premium for modified whole life increases each year after the first few years of policy issue
    B. the premium for graded premium whole life increases each year during the first few years after policy issue
    C. modified whole life contracts build cash values and have premium-paying periods to age 100
    D. graded premium whole life policies build cash values and have premium-paying periods to age 100

35. A form of whole life insurance that begins building cash values immediately following payment of the first premium is called

    A. modified whole life
    B. graded premium whole life
    C. minimum deposit insurance
    D. term insurance

36. A life insurance policy under which the amount a policyowner pays in during the first years exceeds the sum of net level premiums that would have been payable to provide paid-up future benefits in seven years is called a(n)

    A. paid-up contract
    B. flexible premium contract
    C. modified endowment contract
    D. variable contract

37. Which of the following statements regarding modified endowment contracts (MECs) is correct?

    A. The tax treatment of MECs is like any other life insurance policy.
    B. Congress has granted the MEC the most favorable tax status among all life insurance policies.
    C. To avoid being classified as a MEC, a life insurance policy must satisfy the 7-pay test.
    D. According to the 7-pay test, if the total amount a policyowner pays into a life contract during its first seven years is less than the sum of the net level premiums that would have been payable to provide paid-up future benefits in seven years, the policy is a MEC.

38. All of the following statements pertaining to a 20-year family term insurance policy are correct EXCEPT

    A. it usually is sold in units, each valued at ten dollars or more
    B. it is a policy of decreasing term insurance
    C. if the insured dies during the 20-year term period, the monthly income is paid to the family for 20 years, starting at the time of death
    D. when the insured dies, the family generally may take the commuted value of the policy in cash in lieu of monthly income

39. Which of the following policy plans provides for payment of an income for a selected, fixed period of years beginning from the date of the insured's death?

    A. Family income
    B. Family maintenance
    C. Family plan
    D. Joint and survivor plan

40. Suppose that two years before he died, an insured bought a policy to maintain his family's income. The policy pays monthly benefits to the family for five years following the date of the insured's death. The face amount of the ordinary insurance portion of the policy is paid at the end of the five-year period. What kind of policy did the insured buy?

    A. Five-year family income plan
    B. Five-year family maintenance plan
    C. Seven-year family income plan
    D. Seven-year family maintenance plan

41. All of the following statements concerning a family plan policy are correct EXCEPT

    A. the policy normally is sold in units
    B. it typically covers all children in a family within certain age limits
    C. it provides both parents with the same amount of protection
    D. it is designed to insure all members of an immediate family in one policy

42. Don and Edith purchase a family plan consisting of four units to cover themselves and their two children. A unit provides coverage of $10,000 for Don, $2,500 for Edith and $2,000 for each child. Total coverage for each parent is

    A. $10,000 for Don and $2,500 for Edith
    B. $12,500 for Don and $10,000 for Edith
    C. $14,500 for Don and $2,500 for Edith
    D. $40,000 for Don and $10,000 for Edith

43. A family in which both parents work and, therefore, are in need of the same amount of coverage, would be a candidate for which of the following plans?

    A. Family maintenance
    B. Family plan
    C. Joint life
    D. Juvenile plan

44. Which of the following statements pertaining to juvenile life insurance is(are) correct?

    A. Ricardo, father of Georgia, age six, has applied for a juvenile policy on his daughter's life. Ricardo will be the policyowner.
    B. Bobby, age eight, presently is the insured in a $5,000 jumping juvenile policy. When he reaches age 21, the policy's face amount automatically will increase to $25,000.
    C. Both A and B are correct.
    D. Neither A nor B is correct.

45. The payor benefit typically waives premiums on a juvenile policy if the

    A. person who pays the premium dies or becomes disabled before the insured child reaches a certain age
    B. policy is converted before the insured reaches a specified age
    C. insured child becomes disabled
    D. insured child dies before reaching a specified age, usually 21 or 25

46. The purpose of juvenile insurance is to

    A. provide funds for a child's final expenses
    B. fund a college education
    C. begin a life insurance program for a child at a low premium rate
    D. do all of the above

47. A significant feature of adjustable life insurance is that the

    A. policyowner may make retroactive adjustments in the policy's provisions
    B. premiums may be increased or decreased from time to time by the policyowner
    C. policyowner need not pay premiums after the policy has been in force for a certain number of years
    D. cash value is three times greater than in traditional whole life insurance

48. Patrick owns an adjustable life policy. Which of the following statements pertaining to his policy is correct?

    A. Upon showing evidence of insurability, Patrick can increase the face amount of his policy.
    B. The company has a right to raise or lower the premium based on its investment earnings.
    C. Any adjustments made on the policy will have retroactive effects on the policy's provisions.
    D. Decreasing the premium shortens the premium-paying period.

49. Which of the following statements is applicable to universal life insurance?

    A. The policy involves a cash account and increasing term insurance coverage.
    B. A rate of interest higher than that paid on whole life is paid for the term of the policy.
    C. Premiums generally may be increased or decreased at the policyowner's option.
    D. It is similar to endowment insurance.

50. Universal life is distinguished from whole life insurance in that

    A. no withdrawals can be made from the policy's cash value account
    B. policy loans can be taken from the policy
    C. partial withdrawals can be taken from the cash value account
    D. complete withdrawals of the cash value can be taken

51. All of the following statements regarding universal life insurance are true EXCEPT

    A. the policyowner has the right to increase or decrease the interest rate credited to his or her cash value account, as his or her needs change
    B. the cost of the insurance protection is taken from the policy's cash value account each month
    C. as long as the policy's cash values are sufficient to support the cost of the insurance protection, the policy remains in force, whether or not premiums are paid
    D. the policyowner has the right to increase or decrease the amount of the policy's death benefit, as his or her needs change

52. Michelle, age 31, just purchased a $50,000 variable life insurance policy. With regard to her policy, which of the following statements is not correct?

    A. Her premium payments will be fixed and level for the duration of the contract.
    B. She directs the insurer as to how her cash values are to be invested.
    C. The cash value growth of her policy will depend on how the investments supporting those values perform.
    D. At her death, her beneficiary may receive more or less than $50,000 in proceeds.

53. Which of the following types of life insurance requires that the agent be NASD-licensed before he or she can sell these policies?

    A. Universal life
    B. Variable life
    C. Adjustable life
    D. All of the above

54. Which of the following statements pertaining to variable life insurance is correct?

    A. The benefits of variable life insurance vary according to the amount of premiums paid.
    B. With a variable life insurance policy, the insurance company assumes the investment risk.
    C. Variable life insurance cannot be proposed in a sales situation unless the proposal is preceded or accompanied by a prospectus.
    D. In a variable life insurance policy, cash values and the death benefit are not guaranteed.

55. Variable universal life policies provide

    A. a flexible premium capability
    B. cash values
    C. a death benefit
    D. all of the above

56. Which of the following life insurance policy options will allow insureds to purchase additional insurance at future dates, regardless of their health?

    A. Guaranteed insurability option
    B. Double indemnity option
    C. Waiver of premium option
    D. Conversion option

57. At the age of 35, Ben purchased a whole life policy with a guaranteed insurability option. How many opportunities will he have to purchase additional life insurance in the future?

    A. Two
    B. Three
    C. Four
    D. Five

58. If an insured does not exercise his or her option to increase coverage under a guaranteed insurability rider, what is the result?

    A. The insurer automatically increases the coverage, per the amount stated in the option.
    B. The policy is canceled.
    C. The coverage will not change and the option automatically expires.
    D. The premiums on the underlying policy are lowered proportionately, since no increase in insurance coverage was purchased.

59. Which of the following statements pertaining to the waiver of premium provision in a life insurance policy is(are) correct?

    A. Beverly was totally disabled for three years. During that time she did not have to pay the premiums on her life insurance policy because it included a waiver of premium provision. Now she is recovered and will never have to repay the company for the premiums waived during her disability.
    B. Dale was totally disabled on June 1. The annual premium for his life insurance policy, which has a waiver of premium provision, is due and payable June 30. Dale need not pay that premium, since the disability commenced before the premium due date.
    C. Grady's whole life policy had a cash value of $3,100 when he became totally disabled. His premiums were waived under the policy's waiver of premium provision. During the 24 months he was disabled, his policy's cash value would have remained at $3,100.
    D. All of the above are correct statements.

60. Jason has been totally disabled for two years. During that time, the company has paid all premiums (a total of $1,200) on his $25,000 life policy, which has a waiver of premium clause. If Jason dies now, the company will pay a death benefit of

A. $12,500
B. $23,300
C. $23,800
D. $25,000

61. All of the following statements pertaining to the waiver of premium provision in a life insurance policy are correct EXCEPT

A. a waiver of premium provision specifies a waiting period of usually 90 days or six months after the disability commences before the waiver takes effect
B. if the policy is participating, dividends will continue to be paid during the continuance of the disability
C. after disability requirements are satisfied, premiums paid by the policyowner during the waiting period are refunded by the company
D. a waiver of premium provision may be continued indefinitely with a policy so long as premiums are paid and the policy remains in force

62. Jay has a $50,000 life insurance policy with an accidental death benefit that pays triple the face amount. If Jay commits suicide three years after purchasing the policy, how much will his beneficiary receive?

A. $0
B. $50,000
C. $100,000
D. $150,000

63. For a beneficiary to receive accidental death benefits, death of the insured generally must occur within how many days following the accident?

A. 30 days
B. 45 days
C. 60 days
D. 90 days

64. The insured in a $25,000 life insurance policy died of a heart attack. Since the policy had a double indemnity provision, the policy beneficiary received

A. nothing
B. $12,500
C. $25,000
D. $50,000

65. The payor benefit option or rider is used with

A. family income insurance
B. joint life
C. juvenile policies
D. adjustable life

66. Which of the following options is designed to protect the policyowner should the policy be in danger of lapsing for nonpayment of premium?

A. waiver of premium
B. guaranteed insurability
C. premium exclusion
D. automatic premium loan

67. Lisa exercised her automatic premium loan provision to pay her annual premium on her $50,000 life insurance policy. She died four months after the loan was taken, never having a chance to repay it. Given these facts, which of the following is correct?

A. The premium was paid by the insurance company from its reserves.
B. The amount paid to Lisa's beneficiary as the death proceeds was reduced by the amount of the loan.
C. The policy was canceled, since the loan was not repaid.
D. The type of insurance Lisa owned was term.

68. Which of the following statements regarding a cost of living rider on a life insurance policy is(are) correct?

    A. A cost of living rider seeks to protect against inflations erosion of life insurance policy values.
    B. An inflation index determines the amount of inflation adjustment that must be made to the policy up to a maximum percentage increase.
    C. Both A and B are correct.
    D. Neither A nor B is correct.

69. Upon the insured's death, which of the following policies will pay the face amount of the policy plus a sum equal to all or a portion of the premiums paid?

    A. Guaranteed dividend policy
    B. Adjusting benefit policy
    C. Cost-of-living policy
    D. Return-of-premium policy

70. What type of life insurance offers relatively small amounts of coverage for individuals who cannot typically afford larger policies?

    A. Group
    B. Industrial
    C. Whole
    D. Family

71. Which of the following kinds of life insurance is most widely used for group plans?

    A. Whole life
    B. Endowment
    C. Limited pay life
    D. Term

72. If the employer pays the entire premium on a group policy, the plan is called

    A. contributory
    B. noncontributory
    C. industrial
    D. convertible

73. All of the following groups would be eligible for group insurance EXCEPT a(n)

    A. labor union
    B. employer-employee group
    C. family of 10
    D. trade association

74. Under a group life insurance plan, each insured person receives a(n)

    A. booklet of information
    B. insurance statement
    C. individual policy
    D. certificate of insurance

Answers & Rationale

1. **B.** Under term life insurance, the option to renew allows the policyowner to renew the policy without evidence of insurability. The renewal is then effected by the policyowner paying the premium for the age then attained, not per the basis of his or her health.

2. **C.** Under a renewable term policy, the premiums remain level for each term period, but increase at each renewal based on the older age of the insured.

3. **C.** Nonrenewable policies are less expensive than renewable policies, all other things being equal. This is because the renewal provision provides continued coverage without evidence of insurability, putting the insurer at greater risk.

4. **A.** Under term life insurance, the option to convert offers the insured the right to change the term policy to permanent insurance without evidence of insurability.

5. **D.** A term policy can be purchased with an option to renew, an option to convert or both. The option to renew allows the policyowner to renew the policy (at the then-attained age premium) without evidence of insurability; the option to convert allows the policyowner to convert the term policy to a permanent type (with an adjustment to premium), without evidence of insurability. Renewable policies carry higher premiums than nonrenewable policies.

6. **B.** The option to renew and the option to convert are available in term insurance for additional premiums.

7. **C.** Level term insurance provides a level face amount of coverage for the term of the policy. Because it covers a specified term only (and does not have a cash value), it is cheaper than whole and limited pay (including single-premium) life. Since the $150,000 amount remains level in this problem, level term insurance is just what is needed.

8. **D.** Level term insurance provides a constant, level face amount of coverage for the term of the policy.

9. **B.** As Peggy died within the ten-year term period, her beneficiaries equally split the $50,000 face amount, each receiving $25,000.

10. **D.** In this case, the insured died after his term policy period had expired. As a result, his beneficiary received nothing.

11. **B.** Level term insurance provides a fixed, level face amount. Decreasing term insurance provides a constantly decreasing benefit amount and carries a lower premium. As a result, Chester's beneficiary would have received $25,000 from his level term policy, and Joel's beneficiary would have received less from his decreasing term policy, had both insureds died within the 15-year term periods. However, if death took place after 1990 (the end of the 15-year term period), neither Chester's nor Joel's beneficiary would receive anything.

12. **D.** Decreasing term insurance is designed to address needs that decrease from year to year, such as mortgage or loan protection. By the end of the term period, the face amount decreases to nothing. This would not help create a retirement fund.

13. **B.** Decreasing term insurance is designed to address needs that decrease from year to year. A decreasing term policy could be written for an amount of insurance to equal the remaining cost of the son's tuition. It would not be used as a method to create funds as would be necessary to fund the daughter's education, nor does it create any cash value which could be borrowed.

14. **B.** Increasing term insurance is used primarily to provide a benefit that increases over time. As such, it is usually sold as a rider.

15. **C.** Credit life is usually sold in the form of decreasing term insurance. In this way, the policy amount decreases to zero when the loan is paid.

16. **A.** The accumulation that builds over the life of a policy is referred to as the policy's cash value, and belongs to the policyowner, who may or may not be the insured.

17. **A.** The cash values of a straight whole life policy can be accessed through a policy loan or through a complete withdrawal of the entire cash value. A policy loan allows the policy to continue in force (though any amount not paid back with interest at the time of death will be subtracted from the death benefit); a complete withdrawal constitutes a surrender of the policy and coverage would lapse.

18. **A.** The cash values of a whole life policy grow steadily and, if the insured lives and premiums are paid to age 100, will equal the face amount.

19. **D.** The face amount of a whole life policy may be paid as a lump sum at the policyholder's death, not at retirement age.

20. **D.** An option to renew is a feature of term insurance.

21. **C.** Upon the death of an insured, a whole life policy pays its face amount. In this case, the face amount is $30,000.

22. **B.** Term policies do not endow (meaning the point when the cash value equals the face amount). Endowment policies can endow at different ages. Whole life and limited pay life endow at age 100.

23. **B.** By design, a whole life policy endows for its face amount at age 100. That means at the policyowner's age 100 the values of his or her policy equal the face amount of the policy. At that point, the insurance is canceled, and the insured receives the face amount as an endowment.

24. **B.** Both limited pay life and whole life policies endow at age 100. A single-premium policy would cost less than a policy with payments spread over its term, since there are fewer administrative expenses involved with single payment policy.

25. **A.** Limited pay life insurance policies have shorter premium-paying periods; the shorter the period, the higher the premium.

26. **C.** Although the premium payments are limited to a certain period, the insurance protec-tion extends until the insured's death, whenever that may be, or to age 100.

27. **A.** The endowment described in this question is a 20-year endowment and, as such, necessitates 20 years of premiums.

28. **A.** The policy described in this question is a 20-pay endowment at age 60. The premiums are payable for 20 years and the policy endows at the insured's age 60.

29. **D.** A 30-year endowment policy provides 30 years of insurance protection.

30. **D.** The policy described is a 20-pay endowment at age 60 policy. In this case, the premium payments are completed 20 years before the time of endowment.

31. **C.** The modified whole life policy is a variation of the traditional whole life policy, not an endowment policy. The premiums in a modified whole life policy are lower in the early years of the policy's term and higher in its later years.

32. **B.** The modified whole life policy is issued with a level premium payable during the first few (usually five) years that is lower than the normal whole life policy rates. The premium increases and are higher than normal thereafter.

33. **C.** Graded premium whole life, like modified whole life, redistributes the policy premiums. The premium is lower than normal whole life rates during the preliminary period following issue (usually five to ten years) and increases each year until leveling off after the preliminary period. A modified whole life policy has a level premium during the preliminary period.

34. **A.** Premiums for modified whole life policies do not increase annually after the first few years. They level off after the premium period.

35. **C.** Minimum deposit insurance begins building cash values immediately following payment of the first premium. Subsequent premiums are paid by borrowing from the cash value.

36. **C.** Primarily to discourage the sale and purchase of life insurance for investment purposes or as a tax shelter, Congress enacted The

Technical and Miscellaneous Revenue Act (TAMRA) that effectively created a new class of insurance—modified endowment contracts (MECs).

37.   **C.**   A life insurance policy avoids being classified as a MEC by meeting what is known as the 7-pay test. This test states that if the total amount a policyowner pays into a life contract during its first years exceeds the sum of the net level premiums that would have been payable to provide paid-up future benefits in seven years, the policy is a MEC.

38.   **C.**   If the insured dies during the 20-year term period, the monthly income would be paid from the time of the insured's death until the end of the remainder of the term, not for a full 20 years.

39.   **B.**   Family maintenance policies use level term insurance to provide for payment of an income for a selected, fixed period beginning at the insured's death.

40.   **B.**   A family maintenance plan, which uses a level term rider, provides for payment of income for a selected, fixed period of years that begins from the date of death. The face amount of the ordinary insurance portion of the contract is paid at the end of the fixed period. In this case, the term for which monthly benefits will be paid is five years.

41.   **C.**   Family plan policies are designed for a one-income family where most of the insurance is placed on the wage earner. The policies are normally sold in units and cover all members of the family.

42.   **D.**   The number of units in a family plan is multiplied by the amount of coverage. As a result, Don receives $40,000; Edith, $10,000.

43.   **C.**   A joint life plan is simply one policy covering two or more persons. Usually, permanent insurance is written.

44.   **C.**   Insurance written on the lives of children, who ordinarily are from one day to 14 or 15 years old, is called juvenile insurance. An adult, usually a parent or a grandparent, applies for, pays for and owns the policy until the child is old

enough to carry the premiums personally. A special kind of juvenile policy, described in answer B, is known as a jumping juvenile policy. This type of policy is issued on a child in units of $1,000, and automatically increases to five times the originally issued face amount when the child reaches age 21.

45.   **A.**   The payor provision provides that in the event of the premium payor's death or disability, premiums on the policy will be waived until the insured child attains a specified age or until the maturity date of the contract, whichever occurs first.

46.   **D.**   Juvenile insurance may provide funds for a child's final expenses, for a college education or to begin a life insurance program for a child, at relatively low premium rates. Juvenile insurance also can ensure a child has some life insurance if he or she becomes uninsurable later.

47.   **B.**   An adjustable life policy is simply a whole life policy with adjustable features, such as premiums that may be increased or decreased from time to time by the policyowner. Such adjustments cannot be made retroactively.

48.   **A.**   Adjustable life is a whole life policy with adjustable features. Premiums may be increased or decreased at the policyowner's request as can the face amount of the policy (usually subject to evidence of insurability). None of the changes made in an adjustable life policy has any retroactive effect on any of the provisions; adjustments apply only to the future. Increasing the premiums could lengthen the coverage period or shorten the premium-paying period. Decreasing the premiums reduces cash values, shortens the protection period or lengthens the premium-paying period.

49.   **C.**   Universal life insurance functions as whole life insurance, but is essentially level or decreasing term insurance plus an investment account. It matches a client's needs in that he or she can adjust premium payments, the face amount of the policy, or both. Interest is based on the greater of the current rate or the guaranteed policy minimum.

50.   **C.**   A factor that distinguishes universal life from whole life is that partial withdrawals can

be made from the policy's cash value account. Whole life insurance allows a policyowner to tap cash values only through a policy loan or a complete cash surrender of the policy's cash values, in which case the policy terminates.

51.   **A.**   With a universal life insurance policy, an insured can increase the death benefit of the policy as needs dictate; no new policy is issued. Premium payments may be increased, decreased or skipped altogether as long as the cash values are sufficient to pay the monthly premiums. The death benefit is not reduced when premiums are paid from cash values. The amount of interest credited to the policy is the guaranteed rate plus any excess earned.

52.   **D.**   A variable life insurance policy invests its cash values in securities at the owner's direction. There are no guarantees as to the cash value growth or accumulation. Although the death benefit may fluctuate in response to the cash values, a minimum death benefit—the policy's face amount—is guaranteed. Premiums are fixed and payable over the life of the policy.

53.   **B.**   To sell variable life insurance, an individual must hold a life insurance producer's license and a National Association of Securities Dealers (NASD) registered representative's license.

54.   **C.**   Because variable life insurance is considered a security, a prospectus must precede any sale of it.

55.   **D.**   Variable universal life combines many characteristics of variable life (such as a death benefit and an equities-based cash value) with universal life (such as flexible premium payments and adjustable death benefits).

56.   **A.**   The guaranteed insurability option (or rider) permits the insured, at stated intervals, to buy specified amounts of additional insurance, without evidence of insurability. The option requires an additional premium and is usually attached to a permanent life policy at the time of purchase.

57.   **A.**   Typically, the guaranteed insurability option allows the insured to purchase additional insurance at three-year intervals between ages 25

and 40. In this case, Ben would be able to exercise this option at age 37 and at age 40.

58.   **C.**   When no purchase is made under a guaranteed insurability option, the option for that particular age expires automatically; there is no change in the underlying policy. Normally, the insured will have 90 days in which to exercise an optional purchase.

59.   **A.**   The waiver of premium provision provides that if the insured is totally disabled, and after a waiting period of 90 days or six months, the policyowner is relieved of paying premiums as long as the disability continues. Death benefits remain the same and cash values continue to grow, just as if the insured were paying premiums regularly. In selection B, the 90-day (or longer) waiting period had not expired, so the insured must continue to pay the premium during that time. However, if the disability continues, all of the premiums paid by the insured after the disability commenced are refunded.

60.   **D.**   Although premiums are waived due to the waiver of premium clause, the death benefit ($25,000) remains the same.

61.   **D.**   A waiver of premium clause generally remains in effect until the insured reaches a specified age, such as 60 or 65.

62.   **B.**   Suicide is excluded from coverage under the accidental death benefit and, as a result, does not qualify for the additional payment.

63.   **D.**   For a beneficiary to receive accidental death benefits, death of the insured generally must occur within 90 days following an accident.

64.   **C.**   Under a double indemnity provision, the policy beneficiary would receive double the face amount in the event of a fatal accidental injury. Since the insured's death was not due to an accident, the policy paid its $25,000 face amount.

65.   **C.**   The juvenile policy's payor benefit rider provides that the policy premiums will be waived if the person paying the premium dies or becomes totally disabled.

66.   **D.**   Under the automatic premium loan provision, the cash values will be used to pay the

premium if the premium due has not been paid by the end of the grace period.

67. **B.**   The policyowner's cash values are used to pay premium loans. If the loan is not repaid at the time of the insured's death, the amount plus interest is subtracted from the death proceeds.

68. **C.**   A cost-of-living (COL) or cost-of-living adjustment (COLA) rider is tied to an increase in an inflation index, most commonly the Consumer Price Index (CPI). The COL rider provides for automatic increases in the policy death benefit in proportion to increases in the CPI.

69. **D.**   Return-of-premium policies promise to pay the policy face amount plus a sum equal to all or a portion of the premiums paid. Usually the return is limited to premiums paid during a stated period, such as ten or 15 years, or to a stated age, such as 60. Of course, these policies are more expensive than those that do not have a return-of-premium guarantee.

70. **B.**   Industrial life is often called burial insurance because of its small policy limits and corresponding small premiums.

71. **D.**   Most group life insurance plans offer term insurance because of the lower cost factor to the employer.

72. **B.**   When the employer pays the whole premium for a group life insurance plan, it is called noncontributory.

73. **C.**   Family members are not considered groups for the purposes of group insurance.

74. **D.**   Under a group life insurance plan, each person receives a certificate of insurance. The employer receives the actual policy and is the policyholder.

6

PREMIUMS AND PROCEEDS

Basic Premium Factors •
Modes of Premium Payment •
Substandard Premiums • *Tax Treatment*

1. What tool do life insurance actuaries use to help establish premium rates based on the probabilities of death at various ages?

   A. Morbidity table
   B. Mortality table
   C. Survivor table
   D. Annuity table

2. A mortality table reflects

   A. the average life-span for any given individual
   B. who among a given group of individuals will die within a given year
   C. the average number of deaths that will occur in a given year for a given age group of individuals
   D. the declining probability of death as the age of a given group of individuals increases

3. If, out of a starting group of 100,000 individuals, 89,666 are living at age 50 and 602 are expected to die within the year, what is the death rate for that particular age group?

   A. 6.02
   B. 6.71
   C. 8.90
   D. 10.94

4. In the life insurance business, a word that is synonymous with expenses is

   A. underwriting
   B. loading
   C. actuary
   D. controlling

5. All of the following statements pertaining to life insurance premiums are correct EXCEPT

   A. an insurance company invests the premium money it collects to earn interest
   B. in establishing premium rates, a company must assume it will earn a high rate of interest on its invested premiums
   C. the expense factor in premium rate-making frequently is referred to as loading
   D. for an insurance company, the costs of doing business must be reflected in its premiums

6. An insurer invests the premiums it receives in order to earn interest. Which of the following statements regarding this interest factor is(are) correct?

   A. It is factored into the premium rates the insurer charges, which keeps those rates lower than they would be if there were no interest earnings.
   B. The rate of return the insurer earns on its invested premiums is the rate it guarantees its policies will pay.
   C. Both A and B are correct.
   D. Neither A nor B is correct.

7. Which of the following statements pertaining to life insurance premiums is(are) correct?

   A. Bob, who is substantially overweight, has applied for a life insurance policy. His weight may affect his insurability, but not the amount of the premium on his policy.
   B. Harold and Billy, both age 25, each buy a whole life policy from the same company. However, Harold has a participating policy, while Billy's policy is nonparticipating. Harold will pay a higher premium.
   C. Both A and B are correct.
   D. Neither A nor B is correct.

8. Which of the following age groups normally experiences the largest number of deaths in a year?

   A. 20-year-olds
   B. 30-year-olds
   C. 40-year-olds
   D. 50-year-olds

9. All of the following are basic premium factors EXCEPT

   A. the insurer's expenses
   B. interest earnings
   C. the insured's age
   D. the mortality rate

10. All of the following can affect directly the amount of premium an individual insured pays EXCEPT

    A. occupation
    B. sex
    C. age
    D. marital status

11. Assume the following persons buy identical life insurance policies from the same company. Who would pay the lowest premium rate?

    A. Linda, age 30
    B. Thomas, age 30
    C. Brandon, age 34
    D. Arthur, age 42

12. Which of the following types of life insurance policies would have premiums that are fixed and level, and payable over the life of the policy?

    A. Life paid-up at 50
    B. 10-year renewable term
    C. Both A and B
    D. Neither A nor B

13. Ben is considering the purchase of a $75,000 whole life policy. Which of the following options would tend to lower his premiums?

    A. The addition of a guaranteed insurability rider
    B. The waiver of premium option
    C. Paying premiums annually as opposed to monthly
    D. All of the above

14. A life insurance gross premium is

    A. net single premium plus mortality
    B. interest plus expense less mortality
    C. net single premium plus expense
    D. mortality costs plus loading

15. When establishing premiums, insurers express the rate as a

    A. percentage of the policy's face amount
    B. flat rate per risk
    C. cost per insured individual
    D. cost per $1,000 of face amount

16. Which of the following could influence an applicant's mortality?

    A. Hazardous occupation
    B. Personal habits
    C. Dangerous hobby
    D. All of the above

17. The annual premium on Rhoda's life insurance policy came due December 31, 1997. She paid the premium, which was for

    A. 1996
    B. 1997
    C. 1998
    D. any year she designates

18. What is the most common approach for rating life insurance applicants who are determined to be substandard risks?

    A. Issuing a policy in the amount applied for, with a higher than standard premium.
    B. Issuing a policy of less than applied for, with a lower than standard premium.
    C. Issuing a policy in the amount applied for, but reducing the amount paid out as a death benefit.
    D. Issuing a policy in the amount applied for, but crediting its values with lower interest rates.

19. The funds set aside by an insurer to cover future claims on its life insurance policies is known as the

    A. guaranty fund
    B. reserve
    C. surplus
    D. asset account

20. What settlement option is designed to pay out a specified amount of income at regular intervals, over a period of time that varies according to the income amount?

    A. Fixed period option
    B. Interest-only option
    C. Life income option
    D. Fixed amount option

21. Suppose Max wanted to arrange the distribution of his life insurance proceeds so that his wife, as beneficiary, would receive monthly payments for as long as she lived. Which of the following settlement options would meet this need?

    A. Fixed period option
    B. Fixed amount option
    C. Interest-only option
    D. Life income option

22. As beneficiary, Kathryn receives $375 monthly from her deceased husband's life insurance under a fixed amount option. Each payment consists partly of principal (proceeds) and partly of interest. How is this income taxed?

    A. Each payment is received fully tax free.
    B. The portion of each payment consisting of principal is taxed; the remainder is tax free.
    C. The portion of each payment consisting of interest is taxed; the remainder is tax free.
    D. Each payment is fully taxed.

23. In which of the following situations would premium payments be tax deductible?

    A. Randy is the owner and premium payer of a life insurance policy covering his wife, Ellen.
    B. Janet is the owner and premium payer of a mortgage policy that covers the outstanding mortgage on her home.
    C. The ABC Company provides $25,000 of life insurance coverage to each of its 15 employees and pays the full premium.
    D. The ABC Company is the owner and premium payer of a $250,000 key executive policy covering the life of its president.

24. With regard to the taxation of life insurance policies, which of the following statements is(are) correct?

    A. Amy owns a participating life insurance policy on her own life. She can deduct the premium payments, but she will be taxed on any dividends the policy may pay.
    B. Terry owns a 10-year-old whole life insurance policy which she surrenders for cash. She will be taxed on the full amount she receives, since the policy did not mature.
    C. Both A and B are correct.
    D. Neither A nor B is correct.

25. Which of the following settlement options produces benefits that are income tax exempt to life insurance beneficiaries?

    A. Fixed-amount benefits
    B. Lump-sum payments
    C. Fixed-period benefits
    D. Interest-only payments

26. Archibald surrenders a life insurance policy and receives a lump-sum cash payment of $32,000. His premium payments up to the time of surrender amounted to $26,000. How is the surrender treated for tax purposes?

    A. The full $32,000 is received tax free.
    B. Archibald will receive $6,000 tax free and will be taxed on his $26,000 cost basis.
    C. Archibald will receive his $26,000 cost basis tax free and will be taxed on $6,000.
    D. The full $32,000 is taxable as ordinary income.

27. Renee is the owner and insured of a $100,000 policy. She sells the policy to her business partner, Jill, for $35,000 and for the next ten years, Jill pays the $1,200 annual premium. Assuming Renee dies 10 years after the transfer and the $100,000 is paid to Jill, how are the proceeds taxed under the transfer-for-value rule?

    A. Jill receives the $100,000 tax free.
    B. Jill will be taxed on $65,000—the difference between what she paid for the policy and the proceeds she received.
    C. Jill will be taxed on $53,000—the difference between what she paid for the policy plus the premiums she paid, and the proceeds she received.
    D. Jill will be taxed on the $100,000—the transfer-for-value rule makes policies sold for consideration fully taxable.

28. Assume Silo, Inc., provides each of its 20 employees with $50,000 in group term life insurance coverage. Which of the following statements is(are) correct?

    A. Silo, Inc. can deduct the cost of premiums as a business expense.
    B. Each Silo employee must report his or her proportional share of the premium as income.
    C. Both A and B are correct.
    D. Neither A nor B is correct.

Answers & Rationale

1.   B.   A mortality table is used to help establish life insurance premium rates, since it helps actuaries predict the number of deaths—and thus, the number of insurance claims—an insurer could expect to experience in any given year. Morbidity tables predict disabilities.

2.   C.   A mortality table reflects the average number of deaths that will occur in a certain year for a given group of people. Mortality is the relative incidence of death within a given group.

3.   A.   The death rate, also known as the prediction of mortality, is expressed as the average number of people per 1,000 of a given age group expected to die within a year. Thus, 602 divided by 100,000 equals a rate of 6.02 per 1,000.

4.   B.   Each premium an insurer charges must carry its small proportion of normal operating expenses. The expense factor is computed and included in the premium rates for life insurance. The expense factor is also called the loading charge.

5.   B.   A company must remain conservative (low) in its interest earnings assumption. The company is committed to the interest rate it guaranteed its policies will pay.

6.   A.   The interest the insurer earns on invested premiums is factored into the premium rates it charges, so that the rate charged is lower than it would be if no interest earnings were assumed. The rate of interest the insurer earns on invested premiums is not the rate it guarantees on its policies. In fact, insurers hope the return they earn will be higher than what they pay, in order to realize a profit.

7.   B.   Participating policies pay dividends. A higher premium must be charged for a participating policy since it provides dividends. Insurability, as affected by the overweight applicant in option A, directly affects premium amounts.

8.   D.   For obvious reasons, older people die in greater proportions. Thus, the older the age group, the higher the death rate for that group.

9.   C.   Three basic factors must be considered when computing the premium rate for a life insurance policy: mortality (the event or risk the insured wants to protect against); interest (the amount assumed will be earned on the insurers funds); and expenses (the overhead charges the insurer incurs).

10.   D.   For any one individual, occupation, age and sex are factors considered in developing a life insurance premium. Marital status is not, since it does not directly affect a person's proposed life span.

11.   A.   Since female mortality rates are generally lower than those for males, a 30-year-old woman would pay less for life insurance than a 30-year-old man.

12.   B.   Both the life paid-up at 50 and the 10-year renewable term have fixed, level premiums; however, with the life paid-up at 50, though the coverage extends to the insured's age 100, premiums cease when he or she is 50. The 10-year renewable term would require premium payments for the full 10-year period, after which the coverage would end unless renewed.

13.   C.   The less frequently premiums are collected on a life insurance policy, the less it costs the insurer to administer that policy and the more the insurer will have to invest. Consequently, an annual premium payment mode would be less expensive than a monthly premium payment mode. Options that add value to a policy, like guaranteed insurability and waiver of premium, would tend to increase the cost of the policy.

14.   C.   A life insurance gross premium is the amount a policyowner is expected to pay. It is made up of the single amount needed to fund the future benefit (net single premium) and normal operating costs associated with providing coverage (expense).

15.   D.   Premium rates for life insurance are expressed as an annual cost per $1,000 of face amount. Thus, if the cost is $12 per $1,000, the annual premium for a $50,000 policy would be $600 ($12 × 50).

16.   D.   Those employed in hazardous occupations pose a greater risk to an insurer, as do those who engage in dangerous hobbies, such as sky-diving. Habits such as smoking or overeating can also increase the risk of death.

17.   **C.**   All life insurance premiums are payable in advance. Thus, a premium due on December 31, 1997 will be applied to 1998.

18.   **A.**   The most common approach to rating insurance applicants is to issue the policy with a higher than standard premium. The higher premium rate may be permanent or temporary, depending on the type of additional risk the applicant poses to the insurer. Answer C is a loose variation of the old lien system of rating, which is rarely used today.

19.   **B.**   The reserve is the amount, when combined with future premiums and interest, that will be used to cover an insurer's death claims. A life insurer's reserve is considered a liability, because it represents an obligation the insurer must fulfill.

20.   **D.**   The fixed amount settlement option provides for the payment of a policy's death benefit in specified amounts at regular intervals. The duration of the payments is not specified; payments are made until the proceeds—or principal—and interest are exhausted.

21.   **D.**   The life income option provides for the guaranteed payment of the proceeds for the life of the beneficiary.

22.   **C.**   The monthly payment to the beneficiary under the fixed amount option is considered a partially taxable installment (similar to an annuity payment). A fixed, unchanged portion of each payment is considered a return of principal, and

thus, tax free. The balance, however, is taxable as interest income.

23.   **C.**   Premiums paid by a company for group term life insurance are deductible as a business expense, assuming the group plan and its provisions meet the necessary requirements. Premiums paid for personal life insurance are not tax deductible, including key person insurance.

24.   **D.**   Premium payments for personal life insurance are not deductible and dividends paid on participating policies are not taxable. Policy surrenders are taxable only to the extent that amounts received exceed total premiums paid by the policyowner.

25.   **B.**   The lump-sum payment settlement option produces death benefits that are income tax exempt to life insurance beneficiaries. The other options involve interest earned on the proceeds, which is not tax exempt.

26.   **C.**   Archibald will be taxed on the amount that exceeds the $26,000 he paid into the policy, his cost basis.

27.   **A.**   The transfer-for-value rule states that if a policy is transferred for consideration and the insured dies, the transferee will be taxed on the excess of the proceeds over the consideration, including any premiums. However, this rule does not apply to transfers to a partner of the insured.

28.   **A.**   The cost of the first $50,000 of employer-provided group term life insurance coverage is not taxable to the employee and it is deductible by the employer.

7

LIFE INSURANCE POLICY PROVISIONS

Required Standard Provisions • Exclusions • Nonforfeiture Options •
Dividend Options • Beneficiaries • Settlement Options •
Group Life Policy Provisions

1. Which provision of a life insurance policy declares that the application is part of the contract?

   A. Insuring clause
   B. Ownership clause
   C. Entire contract clause
   D. Incontestable clause

2. Which of the following statements is(are) correct?

   A. If an insuring company revises its bylaws or practices, any life insurance contract issued prior to the change must be modified to reflect the company's new policies.
   B. After a policy is delivered to and accepted by the policyowner, it cannot be changed in any way, except in accordance with terms stated in the contract.
   C. Both A and B are correct.
   D. Neither A nor B is correct.

3. All of the following statements pertaining to the insuring clause in a life insurance policy are correct EXCEPT

   A. it specifies how much the company will pay and when payment will be made
   B. it is usually the first clause in a life insurance policy
   C. it names the insured
   D. it gives the policyowners the right to return the policy if not satisfied

4. Further, the Company agrees to pay the surrender value to the owner if the insured is alive on the maturity date. This is an example of a(n)

   A. consideration clause
   B. insuring clause
   C. surrender clause
   D. entire contract clause

5. Which of the following statements pertaining to the incontestable clause in a life insurance policy is NOT true?

   A. The policyowner-insured of a $100,000 life insurance policy died of a heart attack four months after taking out the policy. The company then learned that the insured had been treated for a heart condition nine months prior to being insured, but that fact was omitted from the application. The company had to pay the death benefit because the discrepancy was not uncovered before the insured's death.

   B. An insurer discovers a material misstatement in the application for a life insurance policy it issued five years ago. The company cannot cancel the policy or change it in any way because the contestable period normally would have expired.

   C. The insured in a policy issued September 30, 1994, which includes a two-year incontestable clause, died September 18, 1997. The contestable period in this policy had expired.

   D. Although the company has the right to question the statements in any application, the incontestable clause limits the time in which the company has that right.

6. All of the following statements pertaining to the incontestable clause in a life insurance policy are correct EXCEPT

   A. the clause applies to all policy provisions, including accidental death

   B. it gives reassurance to the policyowner

   C. if the insured lives beyond the incontestable period, the company cannot later contest the policy for misrepresentation so long as the premiums are paid

   D. the specified period after which an insurer cannot contest a policy is usually two years after policy issue

7. All of the following represent circumstances in which an incontestable clause would NOT apply EXCEPT

   A. impersonation of the applicant by another

   B. no insurable interest

   C. intent to murder

   D. concealment of smoking

8. Which of the following statements pertaining to the suicide clause in a life insurance policy is NOT correct?

   A. The insured with a $75,000 life insurance policy issued December 15, 1991, committed suicide December 24, 1993. The beneficiary of the policy received a return of the premiums paid for the policy.

   B. The suicide clause is designed to protect the insuring company.

   C. An insured committed suicide on February 1, 1993. The insured had a $35,000 life insurance policy issued January 28, 1991. The $35,000 death benefit was paid to the beneficiary of the policy.

   D. The suicide clause stipulates a period of time during which benefits will not be paid if the insured commits suicide.

9. Vivian commits suicide four years after taking out a $30,000 life insurance policy on herself. Her beneficiary is concerned that the death claim will be denied. In this case, all of the following are correct statements EXCEPT

   A. the suicide clause in Vivian's policy would have expired, so it would not affect the death claim

   B. the company has definite proof of the cause of her death, so it can refuse to pay the death benefit

   C. if the suicide clause were in effect, the company would refund the premiums paid

   D. if the beneficiary were familiar with the policy's suicide clause, he or she would not doubt payment of the claim

10. Which of the following is stated in the consideration clause of a life insurance policy?

    A. Age of the insured
    B. Insured's general physical condition
    C. Policyowner's occupational classification
    D. Amount and frequency of premium payments

11. Joshua returns to the agent the new life insurance policy delivered by the agent three days earlier. Joshua had paid the initial premium. Assuming his policy has a free-look provision, what is Joshua entitled to receive?

    A. The policy's cash surrender value
    B. One-half of the initial premium as a refund
    C. A credit that can be applied to the purchase of another policy
    D. None of the above

12. Janet, the insured, dies during a grace period for her $50,000 life policy. What happens, considering that her premium has not been paid?

    A. The premium is canceled because the insured died during the grace period.
    B. The amount of the premium due is deducted from the policy proceeds paid to the beneficiary.
    C. The premium due, plus a 10 percent penalty, is charged against the policy.
    D. The beneficiary must pay the premium after the death claim is paid.

13. Which of the following provisions of a life insurance contract generally helps to keep policies in force if policyowners neglect to pay their premiums?

    A. Grace period
    B. Automatic premium loan
    C. Both A and B
    D. Neither A nor B

14. Edna stopped paying premiums on her permanent life insurance policy seven years ago though she never surrendered it. She is still insurable and has no outstanding loan against the policy. The company probably will decline to reinstate the policy because the time limit for reinstatement has expired. The limit usually is

    A. 60 to 90 days
    B. 6 months to 18 months
    C. one year
    D. three or five years

15. All of the following statements pertaining to reinstating a life insurance policy are correct EXCEPT

    A. all back premiums must be paid
    B. any outstanding policy loan must be repaid
    C. the insured must provide evidence of insurability
    D. the cash surrender value must be forfeited to the insurer

16. All of the following statements pertaining to reinstatement of a life insurance policy are correct EXCEPT

    A. a suicide exclusion period is renewed with a reinstated policy
    B. when reinstating a policy, the company must charge the policyowner for past-due premiums
    C. when reinstating a policy, the company must charge the policyowner for interest on past-due premiums
    D. a new contestable period becomes effective in a reinstated policy

17. All of the following are rights of policy ownership EXCEPT

    A. selecting a settlement option
    B. changing a policy provision with the agent's approval
    C. selecting a nonforfeiture option
    D. designating beneficiaries

18. All of the following are life insurance policyowners' rights EXCEPT the right to

    A. name a beneficiary irrevocably
    B. change the mode of premium payment
    C. change the grace period
    D. take a policy loan

19. All of the following statements pertaining to life policy assignment are correct EXCEPT

    A. to secure a loan, the policy temporarily can be transferred to the lender as security for the loan
    B. the policyowner must obtain approval from the insurance company before a policy can be assigned
    C. the life insurance company assumes no responsibility for the validity of an assignment
    D. the policyowner must notify the company, in writing, of any assignment

20. Alexandria assigns one of her $10,000 life insurance policies to a bank as collateral for a loan. The assignee is

    A. Alexandria, the insured
    B. the bank
    C. the beneficiary of the policy
    D. the insurance company

21. An assignment in which the assignee receives full control over the policy is called a(n)

    A. collateral assignment
    B. absolute assignment
    C. guaranteed assignment
    D. revocable assignment

22. Which of the following statements pertaining to the misstatement of age provision of a life insurance policy is(are) correct?

    A. If a deceased insured under a $30,000 life insurance policy is found to be younger than the policy showed, the insured's beneficiary will receive $30,000 if the policy's incontestable clause has expired.
    B. The beneficiary of a policy with a $45,000 face amount will receive more than $45,000 if it is found that the deceased insured was older than the policy indicated, and if the policy's incontestable clause has expired.
    C. Both A and B are correct.
    D. Neither A nor B is correct.

23. Abner's age was misstated in his application for a $50,000 life policy. What will the company do when it discovers the error?

    A. The company will amend the application, but no additional premium can be charged.
    B. It probably will void the policy.
    C. It will adjust either the premium rate or the amount of protection.
    D. It will do nothing—the policy cannot be altered in any way after it has been issued.

24. Which of the following policyowner rights relates directly to the cash value of permanent insurance?

    A. Right to change premium mode
    B. Right to assign proceeds
    C. Right to name beneficiaries
    D. Right to take a policy loan

25. Roberta is the insured in a $30,000 life insurance policy for which she pays an annual premium of $700. There is an outstanding policy loan of $2,500. Her last premium due has not been paid and she dies during the grace period. How much will her beneficiary receive?

    A. $26,800
    B. $27,500
    C. $29,300
    D. $30,000

26. Typically excluded from coverage in a life insurance policy would be death from any of the following causes EXCEPT

    A. hazardous occupation
    B. hazardous hobby
    C. war
    D. commercial aviation

27. An insurer received a request March 1, 1997, for payment of a policy's full cash surrender value. Under the laws of most states, the insurer could delay payment until

    A. September 1, 1997
    B. December 1, 1997
    C. March 1, 1998
    D. June 1, 1998

28. The delayed payment provision in a whole life policy provides

    A. that the insured may postpone premium payment if he or she can demonstrate cause
    B. that the insured may postpone his or her initial premium payment for 30 days
    C. that the insurance company may delay payment of the cash surrender value for six months after the policyholder's request for payment
    D. none of the above

29. Lynn elects to surrender her whole life policy for a reduced paid-up policy. The cash value of her new policy will

    A. continue to increase
    B. remain the same as in the old policy
    C. reduce immediately to $0
    D. decrease gradually

30. Basil has a combination policy consisting of $25,000 whole life and a $20,000 term rider. He stops paying premiums and elects to take a paid-up policy, which will be a reduced amount of insurance based on an original face amount of

    A. $20,000
    B. $25,000
    C. $35,000
    D. $45,000

31. John, age 52, has a straight whole life policy and decides to stop paying premiums and take a paid-up policy for a reduced amount. His next policy will be

    A. any type of policy he selects
    B. an annuity
    C. whole life
    D. term insurance

32. A policyowner stops paying premiums on a whole life policy with an accidental death benefit and exchanges the policy for extended term insurance. All of the following statements pertaining to this situation are correct EXCEPT

    A. the term policy will have a reduced face value
    B. the policyowner will have continued protection for a limited period of time
    C. the term policy has no cash value
    D. there will be no accidental death benefit with the new policy

33. Durwood decides to stop paying premiums on his $60,000 whole life policy at age 60, and exchanges it for extended term insurance. What face value will the term insurance have?

    A. $10,000
    B. $30,000
    C. $45,000
    D. $60,000

34. Arnold buys a $25,000 participating whole life policy. He has a definite need for more life insurance, but feels he cannot afford it. Which of the following dividend options would help to solve this problem automatically?

    A. Taking dividends in cash
    B. Applying dividends against premium payments
    C. Using dividends to buy paid-up additions
    D. Leaving dividends to accumulate at interest

35. All of the following are dividend options EXCEPT

    A. buying paid-up additions
    B. applying dividends to premiums
    C. assigning dividends to pay off a mortgage
    D. leaving dividends to accumulate at interest

36. Unlike corporate dividends, insurance policy dividends

    A. are reported on an insured's income tax filing
    B. are the same as marketable securities
    C. are not considered taxable income
    D. are guaranteed to be declared and payable every year

37. Which of the following dividend options produces a result similar to taking dividends in cash and depositing them in a bank savings account?

    A. Using dividends to buy one-year term insurance
    B. Leaving dividends to accumulate at interest
    C. Applying dividends against premium payments
    D. Taking dividends in cash

38. Which of the following statements is correct with regard to policy dividends?

    A. They are issued on nonparticipating policies.
    B. They are a result of favorable operating or investment income.
    C. Though they may vary from year to year, they are guaranteed to be paid each year.
    D. They are not available to insureds after a specified age, such as 60.

39. Roland purchases a life insurance policy and names his wife, Carol, as beneficiary. Roland's children, Sue and Bob, are to share the benefits equally if Carol dies before him. His church is to receive the proceeds if his wife and children all predecease him. The primary beneficiary is

    A. Carol
    B. Sue
    C. Bob
    D. the church

40. Roland buys a life insurance policy and names his wife, Carol, as beneficiary. Roland's children, Bob and Sue, are to share the benefits equally if Carol dies before him. His church is to receive the proceeds if his wife and children predecease him. How would the proceeds of Roland's policy be distributed if both his children predecease him?

    A. Carol would receive 50 percent of the proceeds.
    B. Carol would receive 75 percent of the proceeds.
    C. The church would receive 100 percent of the proceeds.
    D. Carol would receive 100 percent of the proceeds.

41. If a beneficiary has been so designated that he or she acquires a vested right in the policy immediately upon its issuance, the designation is termed

    A. vested
    B. contractual
    C. irrevocable
    D. primary

42. Which of the following statements pertaining to beneficiaries of life insurance policies is(are) correct?

    A. A widower dies. His two sons are named beneficiaries in his life insurance policy. However, one son died previously, leaving two children who are to share equally in their father's portion of the proceeds. This is a per stirpes beneficiary arrangement.
    B. A widow dies. Her two daughters are named beneficiaries to her life insurance policy. However, one daughter died previously, leaving the other daughter as sole beneficiary to receive the policy proceeds. This is a per capita beneficiary arrangement.
    C. Both A and B are correct.
    D. Neither A nor B is correct.

43. Assume Clarence, the insured, designated his estate as the beneficiary to his life insurance policy. Based on that, which of the following statements is(are) correct?

    A. The amount of Clarence's estate will be reduced by the amount of proceeds it receives.
    B. The heirs will be able to select specific settlement options from the estate, just as if they were the direct beneficiaries.
    C. Clarence's creditors can attach the proceeds more readily than if the proceeds were paid to named beneficiaries.
    D. All of the above are correct statements.

44. The beneficiary on Susan's life insurance policy reads, Children of the Insured. Which of the following phrases best describes this type of beneficiary designation?

    A. Juvenile beneficiaries
    B. Class beneficiaries
    C. Generational beneficiaries
    D. Basic beneficiaries

45. Which of the following terms indicates the insured's right to change beneficiaries in a life insurance policy?

    A. Per stirpes
    B. Revocable
    C. Per capita
    D. Irrevocable

46. Ted, the insured in a $75,000 life policy, and his sole beneficiary, Maxine, are killed instantly when their car is struck by a train. Under the Uniform Simultaneous Death Act, to whose estate will the policy proceeds be payable?

    A. Maxine's estate
    B. Ted's estate
    C. Both Ted's and Maxine's estates, equally
    D. The proceeds will escheat to the state

47. Under a common disaster clause in a life insurance policy, it is assumed that the

    A. insured died last, unless the primary beneficiary lives beyond a stipulated period
    B. contingent beneficiary is entitled to the policy proceeds
    C. primary beneficiary died last, unless the insured lives beyond a stipulated period
    D. insured and primary beneficiary died simultaneously

48. Winston, the insured, and his wife, Irene, his sole beneficiary, both died in a hotel fire. Hospital physicians witnessed that Irene lived at least two hours longer than Winston. The life policy had no common disaster clause. Which of the following will likely receive the policy proceeds?

    A. Irene's estate
    B. Winston's secondary beneficiary
    C. Winston's estate
    D. The state

49. A spendthrift clause in a life insurance policy is designed to protect the

    A. insured
    B. insurance company
    C. insured's creditors
    D. insured's beneficiary

50. Which of the following statements pertaining to the spendthrift clause in a life insurance policy is NOT correct?

    A. It is designed to protect beneficiaries against the claims of creditors.
    B. It does not exempt proceeds paid to beneficiaries in a lump sum.
    C. A beneficiary receives $125 per month from a life policy under the fixed-amount settlement option and a spendthrift clause; the beneficiary may have the insurance company send the monthly payments to a creditor to pay off a debt.
    D. The exemption applies only to money held in trust by the insurance company that is payable at some future time to the named beneficiary.

51. Which of the following policyowner rights contribute(s) to the flexibility of a life insurance policy?

    A. Settlement options
    B. Nonforfeiture options
    C. Both A and B
    D. Neither A nor B

52. As primary beneficiary under a cash refund option in a life insurance policy, Jeffrey received $355 per month for five years before suffering a fatal heart attack. The policy's original proceeds amounted to $50,000. Jeffrey's daughter, the secondary beneficiary, will now receive

    A. a lump-sum payment of $28,700
    B. $355 per month, as payments continue in her name
    C. a lump-sum payment of $50,000
    D. nothing

53. Horace wants his $85,000 life insurance policy arranged to pay his wife a monthly income if he dies first, but most or all of the proceeds to go to their two children after her death. Which of the following settlement options could Horace select to provide income for his wife and conserve the proceeds for the children?

    A. Interest-only option
    B. Fixed-period option
    C. Fixed-amount option
    D. Life income option

54. Once a life insurance settlement option has been put into effect, the relationship between a beneficiary and the insurance company is that of

    A. recipient/donor
    B. payee/trustee
    C. creditor/debtor
    D. heir/grantor

55. Which of the following statements pertaining to life insurance policy settlement options is NOT correct?

    A. By using the interest-only option, two or more settlement options can be combined for added flexibility.
    B. Payments under the interest-only option may be made at a rate higher than the guaranteed minimum.
    C. Diane and Rhonda each were receiving monthly income from their deceased husband's identical life insurance policies under the fixed-period option. Diane's payments were to be made for 15 years and Rhonda's for 20 years; thus, Diane received the larger payments.
    D. Under a life income option, income payments will continue as long as the primary beneficiary lives or until the principal is depleted.

56. Under a fixed-period life insurance settlement option, excess interest will

    A. increase the size of the payments
    B. shorten the payment period
    C. have no effect on payments
    D. lengthen the payment period

57. Which of the following statements pertaining to life insurance policy settlement options is correct?

 A. Excess interest reduces the amount of each income payment under a fixed-amount option.
 B. Under a fixed-amount option, the lower the interest rate, the smaller each payment will be.
 C. Selection of a smaller payment will increase the payment period under a fixed-amount option.
 D. Principal and interest are paid over a specified number of years under a fixed-amount option.

58. Which of the following statements pertaining to life insurance policy settlement options is(are) correct?

 A. Under a life income–only option, if a primary beneficiary dies after receiving income payments for only three months, the balance of the proceeds would be paid in a lump sum to the secondary beneficiary.
 B. Glenn and Jerry became primary beneficiaries of life insurance policies when their respective wives died: Glenn under a life income–only option and Jerry under a life income with cash refund option. Jerry's income is based on the higher rate per $1,000 of proceeds.
 C. Under an installment refund option, if the primary beneficiary dies, installments of the same amount continue to the secondary beneficiary until all installments paid to both beneficiaries equal the original amount of proceeds.
 D. All of the above are correct statements.

59. Beth is secondary beneficiary of a life policy, receiving monthly income benefits under an installment refund option. Her mother, the primary beneficiary, received a total of $4,200 in benefits before she died. The original proceeds totaled $22,000. Assuming Beth lives long enough, she will be paid monthly benefits until she has received a total of

 A. $4,200
 B. $17,800
 C. $18,700
 D. $22,000

60. Under an installment refund settlement option, if the primary beneficiary dies, the secondary beneficiary will receive

 A. a lump-sum payment
 B. the same income payments until the total amount paid out to both beneficiaries equals the original amount of proceeds
 C. one-half of the remaining proceeds
 D. the same income payments for a fixed period of years

61. Norris is the primary beneficiary of a life insurance policy. He dies after receiving $275 per month for six years, under a 10-year period certain income option. His son, Neil, is the secondary beneficiary. Which of the following statements pertaining to this situation is correct?

 A. Neil will receive income checks in the same amount as his father for four years.
 B. Neil will receive $275 monthly for as long as he lives.
 C. Neil will receive nothing since Norris did not survive the 10-year period certain.
 D. Neil will receive a lump-sum payment of $13,200.

62. Which of the following period certain income options would call for the highest payment rate per $1,000 of life policy proceeds?

    A. 15-year period certain
    B. 10-year period certain
    C. 5-year period certain
    D. 20-year period certain

63. Hector's wife was the primary beneficiary of his $250,000 life insurance policy. She received payments of approximately $700 a month as long as she lived and at her death, their two children received lump-sum payments of $125,000 each. What settlement option was in effect on Hector's policy?

    A. Life income option
    B. Interest-only option
    C. Period certain option
    D. Installment refund option

64. Doris and Arnold receive $450 per month under a joint and one-half survivor life insurance option. What happens if Arnold should die first after payments are started?

    A. Doris would receive $450 per month as long as she lived.
    B. Doris would have to select another settlement option.
    C. The remaining proceeds would be paid to Doris in a lump sum.
    D. Monthly payments of $225 would be made to Doris as long as she lived.

65. Carl and Laura receive $270 per month under a joint and two-thirds survivor life policy settlement option. What would happen if Carl died within one year after payment started?

    A. The balance of the proceeds would be paid to Laura in a lump sum.
    B. Laura would receive $135 per month for as long as she lived.
    C. Laura would continue to receive a monthly benefit of $270 for as long as she lived.
    D. Laura would receive $180 per month for as long as she lived.

66. All of the following statements pertaining to the conversion privilege of group term life insurance are correct EXCEPT

    A. an insured employee typically has 31 days following termination of employment in which to convert the group insurance
    B. when a group plan is terminated, group coverage of the insureds generally is extended for 60 days
    C. insureds who convert their coverage to individual policies pay a premium rate according to their attained age
    D. a covered individual may exercise the conversion privilege regardless of his or her insurability

67. Group life insurance plans in which employees contribute to the overall premium are called

    A. group underwritten
    B. contributory
    C. participatory
    D. noncontributory

68. Television station KTKT has a group life policy covering its 90 employees, each of whom received a(n)

    A. certificate of insurance
    B. share of stock
    C. individual policy
    D. master policy

69. What is the method used for establishing a premium for group insurance?

    A. Enrollment rating
    B. Group credit rating
    C. Experience rating
    D. Franchise rating

70. All of the following apply to franchise life insurance EXCEPT

   A. franchise plans are commonly used for large groups
   B. under a franchise plan, the type of insurance available to individual members is determined by the sponsoring association
   C. a franchise plan may provide for employer contributions
   D. a franchise plan deviates from the typical group plan in that the employer is not the master policyholder

Answers & Rationale

1.   **C.**   The entire contract clause states that the entire contract consists of the policy and an attached copy of the application, including a report of the insured's physical condition.

2.   **B.**   Because of the entire contract provision, policyowners are protected against arbitrary changes by the issuing company. Issued policies are not affected by later changes of any kind in an insurer's bylaws or practices. The policy can only be changed in accordance with terms spelled out in the contract.

3.   **D.**   The insuring clause is the company's promise to pay. The free-look provision allows the insured to return the policy within a specified time, if not satisfied.

4.   **B.**   The insuring clause defines and describes the scope of coverage provided and limits of indemnification. Keep in mind that the clause is not actually titled as such, but it appears on the cover of the policy.

5.   **A.**   The incontestable clause prevents an insurance company from voiding a contract for misrepresentation after the time period set forth in the clause. This time period is usually two years. Since the company discovered the insured's misrepresentation on the application within the incontestable period, it has a right to contest paying the benefit.

6.   **A.**   The incontestable clause applies to death benefits only. It generally does not apply to accidental death benefits or disability provisions if they are part of the policy.

7.   **D.**   After a policy has been in force for the specified term, the insurer cannot contest a death claim or refuse payment of proceeds for a concealment of smoking. A policy issued under one of the other three situations may be voided at any time, since it would not be considered a valid, enforceable contract.

8.   **A.**   Suicide clauses typically extend two years, during which time the insurer will not have to pay benefits if the insured does, in fact, commit suicide. The insuring company is obligated to return the premiums paid. In this situation, the insured committed suicide nine days after the clause time period expired; therefore, the insurer must pay the benefits to the beneficiary.

9.   **B.**   As a general practice, the suicide clause provides that death benefits are payable in full after the policy has been in force for two years, even if the insured did commit suicide.

10.   **D.**   The consideration clause of a life insurance policy states the amount and frequency of premium payments on a separate schedule within the policy.

11.   **D.**   Under the free-look provision, policyowners have either 10 or 20 days to examine their new life policies. If not happy with the policy, a policyowner may return it to the insurer and receive a full refund of the initial payment.

12.   **B.**   If an insured dies during the grace period of a life policy, the amount of the premium due is deducted from the policy proceeds paid to the beneficiary.

13.   **C.**   The grace period provides additional time—usually 30 days after the premium due date—in which the policyowner can pay the premium. The automatic premium loan allows for the payment of a premium from a loan of the policy's cash value.

14.   **D.**   The policyowner has only a limited period of time (typically three or five years) after discontinuing premiums in which to reinstate a lapsed policy.

15.   **D.**   Paying back premiums and any policy loans, as well as proving insurability, are required before a lapsed policy will be reinstated. The policyowner does not forfeit his or her cash values.

16.   **A.**   When reinstating a life policy, no new suicide exclusion period goes into effect.

17.   **B.**   Owning a life insurance policy provides certain rights and choices. However, changing a policy provision with or without the agent's approval is not one of them.

18.   **C.**   The policyowner has no right to change the grace period. That provision is a con-

tractual clause developed by the insurer according to individual state laws.

19. **B.** A policyowner may assign or transfer ownership of a life policy to anyone without the insurer's approval.

20. **B.** When a life insurance policy is assigned, the recipient of the policy (in this case, the bank) is called the assignee.

21. **B.** Under an absolute assignment, the transfer is complete and irrevocable. A collateral assignment is one in which the policy is assigned to a creditor as security for a debt until the debt is satisfied.

22. **D.** Situations in which the insured's age is in error are covered under the misstatement of age provision. This states that the policy's benefit will be equal to what the premium the insured did pay would have purchased if the age were correct. Thus, the benefit payable is adjusted up or down in proportion to what the premium that was paid bears to the premium which should have been paid. The incontestable clause has no bearing on a misstatement of age.

23. **C.** Because Abner's age was misstated in his application, the company will adjust either the premium rate or the amount of the protection.

24. **D.** A policyowner has the right to take a policy loan based on the cash value buildup in his or her policy.

25. **A.** When a death claim is filed against a life policy, all amounts due on that policy are subtracted from the death benefit. This includes any policy loans, plus interest due, and any outstanding premiums. In this case, $30,000 minus $700 (annual premium owed) minus $2,500 (outstanding policy loan) equals $26,800.

26. **D.** A life policy might exclude death due to piloting an aircraft (a hazardous hobby or occupation), but it typically would not exclude death by a commercial plane accident.

27. **A.** Laws in most states permit insurers to postpone payment for a policy's full cash surrender value for six months.

28. **C.** While rarely used, the delayed payment provision enables the insurer to postpone payment of the cash surrender value for six months after the policyholder requests payment during times of economic crisis.

29. **A.** Once Lynn surrendered her whole life policy for a reduced paid-up policy, the face value is reduced but cash values continue to increase.

30. **B.** A reduced paid-up policy is based on the original whole life policy amount; the term rider amount is not considered.

31. **C.** When a policyowner decides to stop paying premiums and take a paid-up policy for a reduced amount, the next policy will be the same kind as the original policy.

32. **A.** When a policyowner stops paying premiums on a whole life policy with an accidental death benefit and exchanges the policy for extended term insurance, a policy's cash surrender value is used to purchase an amount of term insurance equal to the original policy's face amount. The term insurance will last as long as the cash value is sufficient to pay premiums. An accidental death benefit would not be included.

33. **D.** When a policyowner stops paying premiums on a whole life policy with an accidental death benefit and exchanges the policy for extended term insurance, a policy's cash surrender value is used to purchase an amount of term insurance equal to the original policy's face amount. The term insurance will last as long as the cash value is sufficient to pay premiums. An accidental death benefit would not be included.

34. **C.** Under a participating whole life policy, if an individual needs more life insurance, he or she can use dividends to buy paid-up additions.

35. **C.** There are five common dividend options: taking dividends in cash, applying dividends against premium payments, leaving dividends with the company to accumulate at interest, buying paid-up additions and buying one-year term protection.

36. **C.** Policy dividends are not taxable income because they are considered a partial return of premiums paid.

37. **B.** Of the five common dividend options, leaving dividends with the company to accumulate at interest is the only choice that directly produces interest income.

38. **B.** Policy dividends, issued on participating policies (policies in which the insureds may participate in the operating and investment results of the insurer) are a reflection of favorable operations, investment or mortality results. They are never guaranteed. In fact, most states require life insurance proposals that contain dividend illustrations to state that future dividends are not guaranteed.

39. **A.** When an insured dies, the first person in line to receive the death proceeds is the primary beneficiary.

40. **D.** In this case, the church as tertiary (third) beneficiary would receive proceeds only if and when all primary and secondary beneficiaries predecease the insured. As Carol is the primary beneficiary, she would receive 100 percent of the proceeds.

41. **C.** If a beneficiary is named irrevocably, the policyowner has given up his or her right to change that beneficiary and, unless otherwise specified in the policy, the owner cannot take any action that would affect the right of that beneficiary to receive the full amount of the insurance at the insured's death. This includes taking out a policy loan or surrendering the policy.

42. **C.** Per stirpes and per capita are terms meaning, respectively, by the branch and by the person. A per stirpes designation provides that proceeds are to split in such a way that the share of any deceased beneficiary will go to that person's surviving children. A per capital designation provides that proceeds are to be shared on a named basis; if any named beneficiary predeceases the insured, his or her share will be split evenly among the surviving named beneficiaries.

43. **C.** If insurance proceeds are paid directly to an insured's estate, the size of the estate will be increased by the amount of the proceeds. Settlement options will be lost to heirs, since an estate will distribute its assets in lump sums. Creditors can attach proceeds more readily if they are paid to an estate.

44. **B.** A policyowner may designate a group of beneficiaries without specifying one or more of the beneficiaries by name, through use of the phrase class beneficiaries.

45. **B.** Revocable is a term indicating the insured's right to change beneficiaries in a life insurance policy.

46. **B.** The Uniform Simultaneous Death Act provides that, if the insured and primary beneficiary are killed in the same accident and there is not sufficient evidence to show who died first, the policy proceeds are to be distributed as if the insured died last. Ted's estate would receive the proceeds, since Maxine, the beneficiary, was deemed to have predeceased Ted, and no other beneficiary was named.

47. **A.** Under a common disaster clause in a life insurance policy, it is assumed that the insured died last, unless the primary beneficiary lives beyond a stipulated period (usually 14 or 30 days). If the primary beneficiary does not live beyond that period, proceeds are payable to the insured's secondary beneficiary or to his or her estate.

48. **A.** In light of the witnesses to the deaths in this problem and in the absence of the common disaster clause, Irene's estate should receive the proceeds. She, as primary beneficiary, outlived the insured policyowner.

49. **D.** The spendthrift clause in a life insurance policy is designed to protect beneficiaries from the claims of their creditors.

50. **C.** The spendthrift clause in a life insurance policy is designed to protect beneficiaries from their creditors by providing that the death benefits payable are not subject to creditor claims. This clause applies only while the insurer holds the money, and only to installment payments.

51. **C.** Nonforfeiture options provide help when the insured no longer wants to pay premiums. Settlement options offer a choice of ways in which proceeds can be paid.

52. **A.** Under the cash refund option, the company will pay the difference between the original proceeds ($50,000) and the total payments made

to the primary beneficiary ($21,300). That amount is paid to the secondary beneficiary in a lump sum.

53. **A.**   Under the interest-only option, only the interest on the face amount will be paid to the wife on a regular basis. The face amount ($85,000) will be saved for the children.

54. **C.**   Under a settlement option, the relationship created between the beneficiary and insurance company is that of creditor and debtor since the insurance company is obligated to fulfill the terms of the settlement.

55. **D.**   The life income option provides that income payments will continue as long as the primary beneficiary lives and even if the principal is depleted.

56. **A.**   Under a fixed-period life insurance settlement option, excess interest will increase the size of payments. Insurers may choose to pay interest over and above the guaranteed rate if they have sufficiently high earnings.

57. **C.**   Under a fixed-amount settlement option, selection of a smaller payment will increase the payment periods. Interest rates do not affect the payment amount on a fixed-amount option. Instead, they affect the length of the payment period.

58. **C.**   Under an installment refund option, if the primary beneficiary dies, installments of the same amount continue to the secondary beneficiary until all installments paid to both beneficiaries equal the original amount of proceeds. Under a life income–only option, installments are paid to the primary beneficiary as long as he or she lives, with no return of principal guaranteed. Therefore, this option provides the largest installments per $1,000 of proceeds.

59. **B.**   Under an installment refund option, the same income payments continue to the secondary beneficiary after the primary beneficiary dies, until the entire proceed amount is paid.

60. **B.**   Under an installment refund settlement option, if the primary beneficiary dies, the secondary beneficiary will receive the same income payments until the total amount paid out to both

beneficiaries equals the original amount of proceeds.

61. **A.**   Under a period-certain income option, installments are payable for the duration of that period, whether or not the primary beneficiary lives. In this case, installments are payable for a period of 10 years. Since the primary beneficiary died after six years, the secondary beneficiary will then be paid the same installments for four more years.

62. **C.**   The shorter the period certain, the higher the monthly payment rate.

63. **B.**   The fact that the policy's proceeds—$250,000—were available for distribution upon the wife's death indicates that they had been held and that she received interest payments.

64. **D.**   The joint and one-half survivor life income option provides an income for two people. In this case, the couple, while both are living, gets the full amount; the survivor, half the amount, or $225.

65. **D.**   The joint and two-thirds survivor life income option provides an income for two people: the full amount for the couple, while both are living; two-thirds of the amount for the survivor.

66. **B.**   When a group plan is terminated, group coverage of the insureds generally is extended for 31 days.

67. **B.**   When employees contribute to the premium payable for a group life insurance contract, the plan is called contributory.

68. **A.**   Employee members of the group receive a certificate of insurance. The company, as policyowner, receives a master policy.

69. **C.**   Group insurance involves experience rating, which is a method of establishing a premium for the group based on the groups previous claims experience.

70. **A.**   Franchise life plans are commonly used for small groups whose numbers are less than the minimum required by state law for group insurance coverage.

8 ANNUITIES

Purpose • Benefit Factors •
Types • Income Taxation •
Tax-Sheltered Annuities

1. All of the following statements regarding annuities are correct EXCEPT

   A. an annuity contract provides for the purchase of income
   B. an annuity is based on mortality assumptions and the law of large numbers
   C. annuity payments are guaranteed
   D. like life insurance, an annuity is used primarily to provide income at death

2. A principal function of annuities is to

   A. create an estate
   B. provide for surviving dependents
   C. liquidate an estate
   D. reduce income taxes

3. Annuities are classified by

   A. method of payment (single vs. periodic)
   B. number of lives covered (single vs. joint)
   C. disposition of proceeds (fixed vs. variable)
   D. all of the above

4. Typically, how are annuity payments distributed?

   A. Weekly
   B. Monthly
   C. Semiannually
   D. Annually

5. Which of the following is NOT a factor that determines the annuity benefit amount?

   A. Annuitant's age
   B. Annuitant's sex
   C. Company's expense (loading) factor
   D. Annuitant's tax bracket

6. The time during which funds are being paid into an annuity is called the

   A. annuity period
   B. accumulation period
   C. savings period
   D. paid-up period

7. All of the following are annuity premium factors EXCEPT

   A. medical history
   B. age
   C. sex
   D. assumed interest rate

8. If both an older and younger person had annuity funds of the same amount and simultaneously began to receive monthly payments, which individual would receive the larger payments?

   A. Older person
   B. Younger person
   C. Both would receive the same amount.
   D. The amount of the payment is based on the purchase date of the annuity.

9. If all other factors are equal, which assumed interest rate results in a lower cost to the annuitant?

   A. Lower
   B. Higher
   C. Level
   D. Average

10. The loading factor in annuities takes into consideration

    A. agents' commissions
    B. clerical support
    C. general cost of doing business
    D. all of the above

11. Which of the following statements regarding annuities is NOT correct?

    A. Pure life annuities provide income as long as the annuitant lives; benefits terminate at his or her death.
    B. An installment refund annuity guarantees a specific amount of benefits, payable to the annuitant only; if death occurs prior to total payout, a portion of the premium is refunded to the annuitant's estate or beneficiary.
    C. Annuities that pay benefits in specified dollar amounts are fixed annuities; annuities that pay benefits in relation to units are variable annuities.
    D. An annuity can be classified as immediate or deferred, depending on when benefit payments begin.

12. The annuitant of an annuity can be compared to which of the following with respect to a life insurance policy?

    A. Insured
    B. Policyowner
    C. Beneficiary
    D. Creditor

13. Which of the following statements pertaining to fixed annuities is(are) correct?

    A. Because Brian would like to protect his wife and son against the contingency of his premature death and also supplement future retirement income, he should purchase an annuity contract rather than a life insurance contract.
    B. The total premium cost of a single premium immediate annuity would be lower than that of a single premium deferred annuity.
    C. Both A and B are correct.
    D. Neither A nor B is correct.

14. Which of the following statements pertaining to fixed annuities is NOT correct?

    A. Jason, age 50, would receive a smaller monthly income payment per $1,000 of an annuity fund than George, age 65.
    B. If William and Margaret, both age 42, purchased identical annuities to supplement their respective retirement incomes starting at age 65, William would be paying a higher premium rate per $1,000.
    C. If Sharon purchases a pure life annuity, further payments will not be made to a beneficiary after Sharon dies.
    D. If Karen died after receiving $95 per month from a $15,000 cash refund annuity for 11 years, Karen's beneficiary would receive $2,460 remaining in the annuity.

15. A variable annuity guarantees which of the following?

    A. The amount of the annuity benefit payments
    B. The rate of return credited to the annuity fund
    C. Both A and B
    D. Neither A nor B

16. What type of annuity would provide for at least a minimum interest rate to be credited during the accumulation period, with a current rate, if higher, to be applied for a specified period, such as three years?

    A. Immediate annuity
    B. Variable annuity
    C. Both A and B
    D. Neither A nor B

17. Annuities may be purchased with

    A. a single lump-sum payment
    B. a schedule of fixed payments
    C. a schedule of flexible payments
    D. all of the above

18. If an annuitant has a refund annuity and dies after the annuity income begins, his or her beneficiary will receive

    A. nothing
    B. a predetermined lump-sum cash payment
    C. a lump-sum cash payment equal to the starting annuity fund
    D. a lump-sum cash payment equal to the starting annuity fund, less the amount of income already paid the deceased

19. The following four people each bought a $20,000 single premium immediate annuity. Assuming all four contracts are identical, who will receive payments over the longest time?

    A. Fred, age 60
    B. Marilyn, age 60
    C. Frank, age 65
    D. Jean, age 63

20. Rick purchased an annuity, making a single lump-sum payment on September 1, 1997. His benefits began on October 1, 1997. What kind of annuity did Rick buy?

    A. Immediate
    B. Deferred
    C. Secondary
    D. Continual

21. What annuity payout option provides for lifetime payments to the annuitant but guarantees a certain minimum term of payments, whether or not the annuitant is living?

    A. Installment refund option
    B. Life with period certain
    C. Period certain
    D. Straight life income

22. What type of annuity settlement arrangement stops making payments when the annuitant dies?

    A. Pure life annuity
    B. Cash refund annuity
    C. Installment refund annuity
    D. Period certain annuity

23. James died after receiving $180 monthly for six years from a $25,000 installment refund annuity. His wife Lucy, as beneficiary, now will receive the same monthly income until her payments total

    A. $2,160
    B. $12,040
    C. $12,960
    D. $25,000

24. Which annuity settlement arrangement guarantees to pay an amount equal to the original investment?

    A. Cash refund annuity
    B. Period certain annuity
    C. Installment refund annuity
    D. Pure life annuity

25. Which of the following types of annuity payout options guarantees as a minimum the payout of the entire annuity principal amount?

    A. Cash refund
    B. Pure life
    C. Period certain
    D. All of the above

26. Which of the following statements pertaining to annuity settlement arrangements is(are) correct?

    A. The survivor under a joint and full survivor annuity receives 100 percent of the original joint income.
    B. An installment refund annuity provides that, when the original annuitant dies, the same income will continue to the beneficiary until the beneficiary dies.
    C. Both A and B are correct.
    D. Neither A nor B is correct.

27. All of the following statements pertaining to variable annuities are correct EXCEPT

    A. the rate of growth is variable
    B. the payments to the annuitants are variable
    C. if the net contribution to a variable annuity account is $350 and the cost of one accumulation unit is $87.50, three units would be assigned to that account
    D. during the accumulation period, the number of accumulation units in the account will continue to grow

28. During the accumulation period of a deferred variable annuity, the value of the individual account rises or falls based on the

    A. variable premiums
    B. number of annuitants
    C. investment results
    D. insurer's expenses

29. Mark's variable annuity currently has 2,500 accumulation units. If each unit is valued at three dollars, the total dollar value of his account is

    A. $833
    B. $2,500
    C. $7,500
    D. $8,330

30. Annuity benefits are a combination of principal and interest. As such, what is the status of the portion of the benefit payments that represents a return of principal?

    A. Taxable when received
    B. Not taxable
    C. Tax-deferred until death
    D. Added to the face amount and taxed when received

31. Employees of which of the following generally may participate in a tax-sheltered annuity (TSA) plan?

    A. Public school systems
    B. Professional sports teams
    C. Professional partnerships
    D. Manufacturing plants

32. Which of the following statements pertaining to tax-sheltered annuities (TSAs) is correct?

    A. TSAs are available to any worker not covered by an employer-sponsored retirement plan.
    B. TSAs are available to employees of certain nonprofit organizations.
    C. Fred, a schoolteacher participating in a tax-deferred annuity, will receive his benefits tax free.
    D. Alice, a vice president of a computer software company, will be taxed on her tax-sheltered annuity payments as she draws the benefits.

33. Annuity payments are taxable to the extent that they represent interest earned rather than capital returned. What method is used to determine the taxable portion of each payment?

    A. Exclusion ratio
    B. Marginal tax formula
    C. Surtax ratio
    D. Annuitization ratio

34. When a cash value life insurance policy is converted into an annuity in a nontaxable transaction, the event is generally known as a

    A. rollover
    B. 1035 exchange
    C. modified endowment
    D. pension enhancement

Answers & Rationale

1.   **D.**   Unlike life insurance, an annuity is used primarily to provide income during life; consequently, annuity payments are guaranteed to be paid as long as the annuitant lives.

2.   **C.**   The principal function of life insurance is to create an estate. The principal function of annuities is to liquidate an estate.

3.   **D.**   Annuities are classified by method of payment, number of lives covered, disposition of proceeds and various other methods.

4.   **B.**   Typically, annuity payments are made on a monthly basis to the annuitant.

5.   **D.**   Age, sex, expenses (plus premium contributions, payment cost, interest rate and type of annuity option selected) are factors that determine the annuity benefit. The annuitants tax bracket is not a factor.

6.   **B.**   The accumulation period is that time during which funds are being paid into the annuity, in the form of payments by the contract holder and interest earnings credited by the insurer. The payout or annuity period refers to the point at which the annuity ceases to be an accumulation vehicle and begins to generate benefit payments on a regular basis.

7.   **A.**   Age, sex and assumed interest rate are annuity premium factors; medical history is not. Annuities do not require any medical underwriting for issuance.

8.   **A.**   If both an older and younger person had annuity funds of the same amount and simultaneously began to receive monthly payments, the older person would receive the larger payments since the insurer would expect to pay the older person for a shorter time according to life expectancy.

9.   **B.**   If other factors are equal, a higher assumed interest rate credited to the accumulation units results in a lower investment from the annuitant.

10.   **D.**   The loading factor in annuities takes into consideration the agents' commissions, clerical support and other general costs of doing business.

11.   **B.**   A refund annuity guarantees a specific amount of benefits, which will be paid regardless of whether the annuitant is alive to receive them. If the annuitant dies before receiving this minimum guaranteed benefit, the money is paid to a beneficiary or to the estate.

12.   **A.**   The annuitant can be compared to an insured in a life insurance policy. The annuitant is the person by whose life the contract is measured. Just as life insurance policyowners are often the insureds, annuity owners are often the annuitants.

13.   **D.**   Annuities are designed to liquidate a principal sum over the lifetime of the annuitant. In essence, they protect against an individual outliving his or her income. They are not designed to protect against the uncertainty of death, as is life insurance. Since immediate annuities commence benefit payments shortly after the date of purchase (with less time to accrue interest than a deferred annuity has), the premium cost is higher.

14.   **B.**   Because men have a shorter life expectancy than women, insurers can expect to make annuity payments to men for shorter periods of time. As such, men pay a lower premium rate per $1,000 than do women.

15.   **D.**   Unlike a fixed annuity, a variable annuity guarantees neither the rate of return the annuity fund will earn nor the amount of benefit payments the annuitant will receive. Both are dependent on how well the variable annuity's underlying investments perform.

16.   **D.**   An immediate annuity does not have an accumulation of three years; a variable annuity does not guarantee the rate of return on its funds.

17.   **D.**   Annuities may be purchased with a single lump sum, a scheduled payment or a flexible payment.

18.   **D.**   If an annuitant has a cash refund annuity and dies after the annuity income begins, his or her beneficiary will receive a lump-sum cash

payment equal to the annuity fund, less the amount of income already paid the deceased.

19. **B.** Statistics show that females live longer than males and will probably collect from an annuity longer. (They pay a higher premium than males of the same age.) In this problem, Marilyn (age 60), the younger female, will collect payments for the longest time.

20. **A.** Annuities can be classified as immediate or deferred, depending on when benefits begin. An immediate annuity begins benefit payouts one payment interval following the annuitants initial payment to the company. Immediate annuities are always purchased with a single payment. In contrast, a deferred annuity begins benefit payouts after a period longer than one payment interval.

21. **B.** Also known as the life income with term certain option, this payout approach is designed to pay the annuitant an income for life, but guarantees a definite period of payments. If an individual has a ten-year life with period certain annuity, and receives monthly payments for six years before dying, his or her beneficiary will receive the same payments for four more years.

22. **A.** When an individual owning a pure life annuity dies, no further payments are made. Of the settlement arrangements listed, a pure life annuity generates the largest monthly income.

23. **B.** Under the installment refund annuity, the beneficiary receives the same monthly income (minus payments previously paid to the original annuitant) until the face amount is exhausted. In this case, the original $25,000 annuity fund has paid $12,960, leaving $12,040 for Lucy.

24. **C.** An installment refund annuity assumes that the total annuity fund will be paid to the annuitant, his or her beneficiary, or both. Keep in mind that a cash refund annuity also provides for the full payout of the annuity principal.

25. **A.** Of these options, only the cash refund payout guarantees that the entire annuity principal will be paid out to the annuitant or beneficiary. A pure life option and a period certain option guarantee payments for a certain period of time, during which principal may or may not be fully liquidated.

26. **A.** The survivor under a joint and full survivor annuity receives 100 percent of the original joint income. Under an installment refund annuity, when the original annuitant dies, the same income will be paid to the beneficiary until the full annuity face amount has been paid.

27. **C.** If the net contribution to a variable annuity account is $350 and the cost of one accumulation unit is $87.50, four units would be assigned to the account ($350 divided by $87.50 equals 4).

28. **C.** During the accumulation period of a deferred variable annuity, the value of the individual account rises or falls based on the investment results of the annuity's underlying securities.

29. **C.** A variable annuity with 2,500 accumulation units, each valued at $3, is worth $7,500 (2,500 × $3 = $7,500).

30. **B.** Each annuity payment consists of both principal and interest. The principal amount is made up of after-tax dollars, and is not taxed when paid. The interest amount is taxable as ordinary income.

31. **A.** Employees of nonprofit charitable, educational and religious organizations may participate in tax-sheltered annuity (TSA) plans.

32. **B.** Tax-sheltered annuities are available to employees of certain nonprofit organizations, such as schools. Participants do not pay current taxes on their contributions, but will be taxed on benefits when they are received.

33. **A.** An exclusion ratio is applied to each benefit payment the annuitant receives to determine the amount that is excluded from taxation: investment in the contract is equal to the exclusion ratio divided by expected return. The investment in the contract is the amount of money paid into the annuity. The expected return is the annual guaranteed benefit the annuitant receives, multiplied by the number of years he or she will receive benefits.

34.   **B.**   Section 1035 of the Internal Revenue
Code provides for tax-free exchanges of certain
kinds of financial products, including the
exchange of life insurance for annuity contracts.

9 RETIREMENT PLANS

Qualified vs. Nonqualified Plans • IRAs • SEPs • Keoghs •
Tax-Sheltered Annuities • Qualified Corporate Plans •
Social Security Benefits

1. Retirement plans can be divided into which of the following two categories?

   A. Fixed and variable
   B. Whole and term
   C. Qualified and nonqualified
   D. Independent and funded

2. What entity qualifies retirement plans?

   A Insurance company underwriting the fund
   B. State insurance department
   C. Federal government
   D. Sponsoring employer

3. All of the following statements concerning qualified retirement plans are correct EXCEPT

   A. employer contributions to a qualified plan are tax deductible as a business expense
   B. employer contributions to a qualified plan on behalf of its employees are taxable income to the employees when made
   C. the earnings of a qualified plan are not taxed
   D. employer-sponsored IRAs are considered qualified retirement plans

4. Many of the basic concepts associated with qualified employer plans can be traced to

   A. the Social Security Reform Act
   B. the McCarran-Ferguson Act
   C. the Employee Retirement Income Security Act
   D. none of the above

5. Wendell, age 57, last year withdrew $1,500 from his IRA which consists entirely of pre-tax contributions. In addition to including that amount in his taxable income, he has to pay a penalty of

   A. $50
   B. $100
   C. $150
   D. $300

6. The penalty for premature withdrawal of funds from an IRA is

   A. 5 percent or $50, whichever is less
   B. 10 percent of the account balance
   C. 10 percent of the pre-tax amount withdrawn
   D. $100

7. David is age 40 and single. He earns $45,000 annually as an engineer with a company that has a group health plan but no employer-sponsored retirement plan. If David sets up an IRA, what is the maximum contribution he can deduct from taxes per year?

   A. $1,000
   B. $2,000
   C. $2,250
   D. $4,000

8. Oliver is age 35, married and earning $55,000 annually as a design engineer. His wife is also employed and files jointly. He is covered by his company's pension plan. Therefore, he is entitled to deduct contributions to an IRA of up to

   A. $0
   B. $250
   C. $2,250
   D. $4,000

9. All of the following employed persons who have no employer retirement plan would be eligible to set up an IRA EXCEPT

   A. Miriam, age 26, a secretary
   B. Brent, age 40, a medical technician
   C. Edna, age 72, a nurse
   D. Jack, age 60, a plumber

10. Lee, age 66, is not covered by an employer retirement plan. This year, he will have gross income of $22,000 from investments, $1,500 from working part-time for a former employer and $7,200 from Social Security. The maximum deductible contribution he can make to an IRA is

    A. $1,500
    B. $2,000
    C. $2,200
    D. $3,000

11. Max, age 32, is employed as an architect and earns an annual salary of $55,000. He is covered by his company's corporate retirement plan. What is the maximum amount he can contribute to an IRA?

    A. $0
    B. $1,500
    C. $2,000
    D. $5,500

12. Herbert and Olga have been married 10 years. They have no children and each has a well-paying job. However, neither is covered by an employer retirement plan. What is the maximum amount they may set aside in tax-deductible IRA funds each year for retirement?

    A. $2,000
    B. $2,250
    C. $3,000
    D. $4,000

13. All of the following statements pertaining to spousal IRAs are correct EXCEPT

    A. an eligible working spouse may set up such a plan with a nonworking spouse
    B. the maximum annual combined deductible contribution permitted is $2,250
    C. the annual contribution must be split into two accounts, with a maximum of $2,000 contributed into one account
    D. a spousal IRA contribution must be reported on a joint tax return

14. Rodney, who earns $40,000 annually and does not participate in an employer retirement plan, has a nonworking spouse. They file a joint income tax return. Which of the following statements applies?

    A. Rodney can establish a separate IRA for himself and another for his wife, and deduct annual contributions of up to $4,000.
    B. Rodney can establish an IRA for himself, but not for his wife because she is unemployed. However, because he is married, he can contribute and deduct up to twice the maximum for an individual IRA, or $4,000.
    C. Both A and B apply.
    D. Neither A nor B applies.

15. Acme, Inc. has established a qualified plan that provides retiring employees with a benefit equal to 1½ percent for each employee's years of service, times his or her final pay, as averaged over the last five years of employment. What kind of plan has Acme installed?

    A. Defined contribution
    B. Profit sharing
    C. Stock bonus
    D. Defined benefit

16. Cynthia is scheduled to receive a $36,000 lump-sum distribution from her former employers qualified pension plan and wishes to establish a rollover IRA to avoid paying taxes on the money that year. Within how many days must the rollover be completed to avoid paying taxes?

    A. 30 days
    B. 60 days
    C. 90 days
    D. 120 days

17. Which of the following statements pertaining to IRAs is NOT correct?

    A. June has accumulated $30,000 of pretax dollars and earnings in her IRA, and at age 55 she withdraws $2,500 to take a vacation. She will have to include the $2,500 in her taxable income for the year and pay a $250 penalty.
    B. Bradley has $36,000 of pre-tax dollars and earnings in an IRA when he decides to retire, and he elects to withdraw $8,000 per year. In his first year of retirement, $8,000 will be included in his taxable income.
    C. If Peter inherits $15,000 in IRA benefits from his father, who died in 1994, Peter can set up a tax-favored rollover IRA with the money.
    D. Walter is age 60 and not disabled. If he takes a distribution from his IRA, it is subject to tax as ordinary income, but with no penalty for early withdrawal.

18. An employer with a simplified employee pension (SEP) plan must include all employees who meet every requirement below EXCEPT the condition that employees

    A. received at least $300 annual compensation from the employer
    B. performed services for the employer during at least three of the past five years
    C. participated in either a Keogh or 401(k) plan with that same employer
    D. reached age 21

19. An employer's maximum annual contribution for an employee to a simplified employee pension (SEP) is

    A. the lesser of 15 percent of compensation or $30,000
    B. a flat $30,000
    C. the lesser of 25 percent of compensation or $30,000
    D. 25 percent of compensation or $25,000, whichever is less

20. All of the following statements pertaining to salary reduction SEP plans are correct EXCEPT

    A. salary reduction SEPs allow employees to defer a portion of their pretax income to the plan
    B. salary reduction SEPs are reserved for employers with 100 or more employees
    C. in order to use a salary reduction SEP, a minimum of 50 percent of the employees must make contributions to the SEP
    D. salary reduction SEPs are an alternative to a 401(k) plan, though the same contribution limits apply

21. If an owner-employee's adjusted gross income is $48,000, what is the maximum amount he or she could contribute to a Keogh (or HR-10) retirement plan?

    A. $4,800
    B. $12,000
    C. $14,400
    D. $24,000

22. All of the following should be eligible to establish a Keogh retirement plan EXCEPT

    A. a dentist in private practice
    B. partners in a furniture store
    C. the sole proprietor of a jewelry store
    D. a major stockholder-employee in a family corporation

23. Oliver, a surgeon, earns $175,000 annually. The maximum contribution he may make to his Keogh plan for the year is

    A. $0
    B. $26,250
    C. $30,000
    D. $43,750

24. Which of the following types of plans would fall under the minimum funding rules of the Internal Revenue Code?

    A. Pension
    B. Profit sharing
    C. Both A and B
    D. Neither A nor B

25. The combination of current tax deduction for the employer plus tax deferral for the employee is possible with which of the following types of plans?

    A. Stock bonus
    B. Money purchase
    C. Both A and B
    D. Neither A nor B

26. Section 457 of the Internal Revenue Code establishes rules for deferred compensation plans for

    A. collectively bargained agreements
    B. state and local governments
    C. multi-employer trusts
    D. employee-owned public corporations

27. Which of the following statements pertaining to qualified corporate retirement plans is NOT correct?

    A. The two types of qualified corporate retirement plans are "defined benefit" and "defined contribution."
    B. Contributions to a qualified corporate retirement plan made by the employer are deductible as a business expense.
    C. Ron participates in his company's qualified retirement plan, which will provide a benefit of 2½ percent of his salary for each year he participates in the plan. This is an example of a defined contribution plan.
    D. A defined contribution plan does not have to provide a definitely determinable future benefit to maintain qualified status.

28. The advantages of qualified retirement plans to employers include

    A. favorable tax rules
    B. increased employee productivity
    C. both A and B
    D. neither A nor B

29. Which of the following plans provides for specified amounts going into the plan currently and identify the participants interest and vested balance?

    A. Defined contribution
    B. Defined benefit
    C. Cash arrangement
    D. Deferred arrangement

30. Which of the following plans allows employees to elect to take a reduction in their current salaries by deferring amounts into a retirement plan?

    A. IRA
    B. Keogh
    C. Defined contribution
    D. 401(k)

31. Which of the following statements pertaining to Social Security benefits is correct?

    A. Only individuals who have paid into the Social Security system are eligible to receive Social Security benefits.
    B. Social Security taxes are payable on all of an individual's income from whatever source.
    C. Social Security pays benefits in the event of retirement or death only.
    D. Both employees and employers are taxed to pay for Social Security.

32. To be eligible for death, retirement or disability benefits under Social Security, a worker must be

    A. completely insured
    B. currently insured
    C. fully insured
    D. partially insured

33. Which of the following statements is(are) correct?

    A. Lester, age 25, who recently became totally and permanently disabled, may qualify for Social Security benefits, as long as he is classified as currently insured.
    B. Continuing to work after retirement will have no effect on a retirees Social Security benefits.
    C. Both A and B are correct.
    D. Neither A nor B is correct.

34. At age 65, a fully insured retired worker is entitled to full Social Security benefits. This equals 100 percent of which of the following?

    A. PIA
    B. AMW
    C. MFB
    D. AIME

35. Which of the following is(are) acceptable as a means to fund an individuals IRA?

    A. Flexible premium deferred annuity
    B. Bank time deposit open accounts
    C. Insured credit union accounts
    D. All of the above

36. Which of the following statements is true about a Roth IRA?

    A. Maximum annual contribution is $2,000 or 100 percent of compensation, whichever is less.
    B. Contributions are not deductible.
    C. Only individuals younger than age 70½ can contribute.
    D. Distributions must begin at age 70½.

37. After owning a Roth IRA for six years, an individual takes a distribution. In which case would the earnings on the IRA be taxed?

    A. The distribution is made before age 59½.
    B. The distribution is used to pay costs of a first home.
    C. The distribution is made after age 60.
    D. The distribution is made before age 59½ because of a divorce.

38. Which of the following expenses may be covered by an education IRA?

    A. Costs of a college education
    B. Costs of ground and flight school
    C. Costs of a trade school education
    D. All of the above

39. Arthur and Donna establish an education IRA for their son, Anthony. Although Anthony attends college full time and graduates, the IRA still contains some funds. Which of the following would be the only way for Arthur, Donna and Anthony to dispose of these remaining funds without incurring a penalty?

A. Distribute the funds to Anthony
B. Wait until Anthony is age 30, then roll over the funds to another education IRA for Donna's graduate schooling
C. Substitute their daughter, Mary, as the beneficiary and use the funds to pay for her high school education
D. Withdraw the funds and close the account

Answers & Rationale

1. **C.** Retirement plans can be divided into two categories: qualified, which meet certain IRS standards, and nonqualified, which do not require IRS approval.

2. **C.** Qualified plans are those that meet requirements established by the federal government and, consequently, receive favorable tax treatment.

3. **B.** Employer contributions to a qualified plan on behalf of its employees are not considered taxable income to the employees when they are made.

4. **C.** The Employee Retirement Income Security Act of 1974, commonly known as ERISA, protects the rights of workers covered under an employer-sponsored plan. ERISA imposes a number of requirements that retirement plans must follow to obtain IRS approval as qualified plans.

5. **C.** When prematurely withdrawing pre-tax dollars from an IRA (before reaching age 59½), the individual must include the amount withdrawn in his or her taxable income as well as pay a penalty equal to 10 percent of the amount withdrawn. There are exceptions which allow an individual to withdraw funds before age 59½ without paying a penalty: for a life annuity, to buy a first home, for education costs, disability, or for gifts to estates or beneficiaries. After age 59½, any IRA distribution is taxed as ordinary income with no penalty.

6. **C.** A premature withdrawal is generally taken before the owner reaches age 59½ and carries adverse tax consequences. The penalty for premature withdrawal of funds from an IRA is 10 percent of the pre-tax amount withdrawn.

7. **B.** Because the individual in this problem has no company retirement plan, he is eligible to set up an IRA and deduct up to the maximum amount of $2,000.

8. **A.** A married person loses IRA deductibility entirely when the couples joint income exceeds $50,000, both spouses file jointly, and one or both are covered under a retirement plan.

9. **C.** Individuals must be under age 70½ to be eligible for an IRA.

10. **A.** Only income received as compensation for services is eligible for an IRA contribution. Compensation includes wages, salaries, fees, commissions, tips and bonuses. It does not include retirement income or earned interest. In this case, although Lee earned $30,700 for the year, only $1,500 is compensation. Because Lee is not covered by an employer plan and he is under age 70½, he can contribute and deduct the full $1,500, which—at 100 percent of his earned income—is still less than the maximum limit of $2,000.

11. **C.** Anyone who is under age 70½ and who has earned income may contribute to an IRA, up to an annual maximum of $2,000 or 100 percent of income, whichever is less. It is the deductibility of the contribution that is affected by the taxpayer's earnings and by his or her participation in a corporate retirement plan.

12. **D.** Married couples who work and are without employer pension coverage may establish IRAs and deduct annual contributions up to a total of $4,000.

13. **B.** Spousal IRAs can be established for married couples when one works and the other does not (or the other earns less than $250). A maximum deductible contribution of $4,000 can be made when the working spouse is not covered by an employer's retirement plan. The contribution must be split between two accounts and the couple must file a joint income tax return that shows their respective contributions.

14. **A.** The spousal deduction is available for qualified taxpayers for separate IRA accounts—one belonging to the taxpayer, the other, to the spouse. The maximum deductible amount is $4,000, with a maximum of $2,000 contributed to each account.

15. **D.** A defined benefit plan specifies the amount of benefit promised to the retiree at retirement. It does not specify the amount the employer must contribute; instead, the amount of contribu-

tion that must be made to fund the future benefit is calculated annually to ensure that the plan will have sufficient funds to pay benefits as each participant retires.

16. **B.**   A maximum of 60 days is allowed to complete a rollover to an IRA before the IRS will tax an individual on a lump-sum distribution.

17. **C.**   Only the individual who establishes an IRA and his or her spouse are eligible to benefit from the rollover treatment.

18. **C.**   Participation in additional employer savings plans neither qualifies nor discriminates against an employees inclusion in a SEP plan.

19. **A.**   An employer's maximum annual contribution for an employee to a simplified employee pension (SEP) is the lesser of 15 percent of compensation or $30,000. The plan must include every eligible employee.

20. **B.**   Salary reduction SEPs are reserved for small companies with 25 or fewer employees. SARSEPS had to be established before 1997. As a result of tax legislation, no new SARSEPS can be established; however, plans that were already in place by the end of 1996 may continue to operate and accept new employee participants.

21. **B.**   The current maximum allowable annual contribution to a Keogh retirement plan is the lesser of 25 percent of after-contribution earnings or $30,000. Thus, if an owner-employee's adjusted gross income is $48,000, the maximum amount he or she could contribute to a Keogh plan is $12,000.

22. **D.**   Keoghs are designed for self-employed individuals, not a stockholder-employee in a family corporation.

23. **C.**   The current maximum allowable annual contribution to a Keogh retirement plan is the lesser of 25 percent of after-contribution earnings or $30,000. Thus, if Oliver's adjusted gross income is $175,000, the maximum amount he can contribute to a Keogh plan is $30,000.

24. **A.**   Since a pension plan is designed to provide a definitely determinable future benefit, the employer must keep the plan's funds at an adequate level at all times, subject to minimum funding standards. Since profit-sharing plans promise no specific future benefit, they are not subject to the minimum funding standards (though there must be substantial and recurring contributions to the plan or it will be deemed terminated).

25. **C.**   The combination of current tax deductibility by the employer and tax deferral for the employee is the primary tax benefit of all qualified plans, of which stock bonus and money purchase are two types.

26. **B.**   Section 457 covers rules for the taxation of participants in deferred compensation plans of state and local governments and non-profit organizations. If a plan is eligible under Section 457, deferred compensation will not be included in gross income until it is actually received or made available. Life insurance and annuities are authorized investments for these plans.

27. **C.**   Answer C describes a defined benefit plan: a plan designed to provide a definitely determinable benefit at some future date.

28. **C.**   Qualified retirement plans provide many advantages to employers including favorable tax rules, increased productivity from employees and good public relations with employees and the public.

29. **A.**   The provisions of a defined contribution plan cover amounts going into the plan currently and identify the participant's interest and vested balance.

30. **D.**   The 401(k) plans allow employees to reduce their current salaries by deferring amounts into a retirement plan. These plans are called cash or deferred arrangements because employees cannot be forced to participate; they may take their income currently as cash, or defer a portion of it until retirement, with favorable tax advantages. The deferred amounts are not included in the employee's gross income and earnings credited to the deferrals grow tax free until distribution.

31. **D.**   Social Security was designed to provide benefits to individuals and their families in the event of death, disability or retirement. It can

cover all members of an eligible worker's family, whether or not they themselves have paid into the system. Social Security is funded by a tax on a worker's pay, which is shared equally by the worker and his or her employer.

32. **C.**   To be eligible for death retirement or disability benefits under Social Security, a worker must be fully insured. To qualify as fully insured, an individual must have one quarter of coverage for each calendar year that has elapsed after 1950 up to the year he or she becomes eligible for benefits, with no fewer than six quarters.

33. **D.**   To be eligible for disability benefits under Social Security, an individual must be qualified fully insured, not currently insured. In addition, working has a big effect on a retiree's Social Security benefits. Retirees who continue to work and earn wages after their Social Security benefits begin are limited as to the amount of wages they can receive. If they exceed this earnings limit, their benefits are reduced.

34. **A.**   The PIA (Primary Insurance Amount) is equal to the worker's full retirement benefit. Social Security will pay this amount at age 65 to a fully insured, retired worker.

35. **D.**   All of these funding vehicles are ideal for an IRA. Other acceptable means of funding are bank certificates of deposit, mutual fund shares, face amount certificates, real estate investment trust units and certain U.S. gold and silver coins.

36. **B.**   Although contributions to a Roth IRA are not deductible, interest, dividends and capital gains accumulate tax free. An individual may set up a Roth IRA and contribute to a traditional IRA, but annual contributions to all IRAs cannot exceed $2,000. Unlike traditional IRAs, there is no prohibition on making contributions after reaching age 70½ and distribution need not start at age 70½.

37. **B.**   A qualified distribution is made after the taxpayer reaches age 59½, made to a beneficiary after the taxpayer's death, made because the taxpayer is disabled, used to buy the taxpayer's first home, or used to pay education costs.

38. **A.**   Education IRAs are special investment accounts for funding a college education, including tuition, fees, books, supplies and equipment, and room and board, provided the student attends school at least half-time. Qualified expenses also include those related to graduate level courses.

39. **B.**   Education IRAs are special accounts to fund college and post-graduate study. If a child for whom an account is established does not attend college or if there are funds remaining in an account when the beneficiary turns 30, these funds can be rolled over to another education IRA that benefits another family member (owner, spouse, child, or grandchild) with no penalty. Another child may also be substituted as a beneficiary, though the funds must still be used to pay for college or post-graduate study. Any IRA distributions that are not used to pay for a beneficiary's education expenses will be included in the recipient's income and will be subject to a 10 percent penalty. Therefore, option B is the only correct way to dispose of the funds without incurring a penalty.

10

LIFE UNDERWRITING AND POLICY DELIVERY

Underwriting • Sources of Insurability Information •
Completing the Application • Third-Party Ownership •
Policy Delivery • Group Underwriting

1. Underwriting is a process of

   A. selecting and issuing of policies
   B. determining and establishing premiums
   C. selecting, reporting and rejecting risks
   D. selecting, classifying and rating risks

2. Which of the following terms describes policies issued to men and women based on the same premium ratings?

   A. Neutral
   B. Sexist
   C. Unisex
   D. All purpose

3. With regard to life insurance applications, which of the following statements is correct?

   A. All applications for life insurance must include a medical exam.
   B. The application includes the names of the insured and beneficiary.
   C. Part I of the application deals with the proposed insured's medical history.
   D. Part II of the application deals with the proposed insured's personal and occupational history.

4. All of the following are sources of insurability information about life insurance applicants EXCEPT

   A. Social Security reports
   B. inspection reports
   C. Medical Information Bureau
   D. the application

5. Which section of the application should contain a record of any injuries the applicant may have suffered?

   A. Medical section
   B. Agent's report
   C. Special questionnaire
   D. All of the above

6. If a medical report is required on an applicant, it is completed by

   A. a home office underwriter
   B. a paramedic or examining physician
   C. the agent
   D. the home office medical director

7. When applicable, all of the following forms require an applicant's signature EXCEPT

   A. aviation questionnaire
   B. authorization form
   C. agent's report
   D. application

8. Which of the following statements pertaining to sources of insurability information is(are) correct?

    A. The insurance agent completes the medical report on a life insurance applicant.
    B. Special questionnaires are used to obtain additional information when an extra hazard or risk may be involved, and to replace the application in unusual cases.
    C. Both A and B are correct.
    D. Neither A nor B is correct.

9. Angela, a recent applicant for a $50,000 life insurance policy, failed to state on her application that she suffered a heart attack a year earlier, fearing it would affect her insurability. Angela violated which of the following?

    A. Doctrine of warranties
    B. Doctrine of interpretation
    C. Doctrine of indemnity
    D. Doctrine of concealment

10. Which of the following statements pertaining to life insurance is NOT correct?

    A. The home office underwriter wants to check with a physician concerning an applicant's past hospital treatment for pneumonia, but does not receive a signed authorization from the applicant. The agent likely will be asked to obtain the signed authorization from the applicant.
    B. Kyle wonders if his life insurance policy will be voided when the company learns that his parents died in a train wreck rather than a plane crash, as stated in his application. In this case, the policy cannot be canceled because statements made on the application are warranties and not representations.
    C. The ABC Co. applies for a life insurance policy on the life of its general sales manager. From the standpoint of insurable risk, the application likely will be approved.
    D. Margaret applies for a policy on the life of a friend. From the standpoint of insurable interest, the application probably will be rejected.

11. All of the following statements pertaining to the Medical Information Bureau (MIB) are correct EXCEPT

    A. the purpose of the MIB is to help prevent fraud and to serve as a reliable source of important medical information about insurance applicants
    B. the MIB is organized and supported by private hospitals
    C. applicants for life insurance must be informed in writing that the insurer may make a report on their health to MIB
    D. applicants must sign authorization forms for information from the MIB files to be given to a member company

12. Which of the following statements pertaining to the Medical Information Bureau (MIB) is(are) correct?

    A. Information obtained in connection with life insurance claims is reported to the MIB.
    B. Information obtained by MIB is available to all physicians.
    C. Both A and B are correct.
    D. Neither A nor B is correct.

13. All of the following statements pertaining to inspection reports on life insurance applicants are correct EXCEPT

    A. they help to determine the insurability of applicants
    B. they provide information obtained principally from law enforcement officials
    C. they generally are requested on applicants who apply for large amounts of life insurance
    D. they usually are obtained from national investigative agencies or firms

14. Which of the following statements pertaining to inspection reports and credit reports on life insurance applicants is(are) correct?

    A. The size of the policy being requested generally determines whether an inspection report is ordered by the underwriting department.
    B. Information contained in inspection reports usually is obtained through interviews with employers, neighbors and associates of the proposed insured.
    C. Applicants with unfavorable credit ratings are poor prospects for life insurance.
    D. All of the above are correct statements.

15. Typically, within how many days must an applicant be notified that a credit report has been requested by the insurer?

    A. Three
    B. Seven
    C. Ten
    D. Thirty

16. Which of the following statements pertaining to a life insurance policy application is(are) correct?

    A. An agent must be very specific when listing an applicants occupation on an application.
    B. If an applicant's age is shown erroneously on a life insurance application as 28 instead of 29, this could result in a premium quote that is higher than it should be.
    C. Both A and B are correct.
    D. Neither A nor B is correct.

17. Elaine signs an application for a $50,000 life policy, pays the first premium and receives a conditional receipt. If Elaine were killed in an auto accident two days later

    A. the company could reject the application on the basis that death was accidental
    B. her beneficiary would receive $50,000, if Elaine qualified for the policy as applied for
    C. the premium would be returned to Elaine's family because the policy had not been issued
    D. the insurer could reject the death claim because the underwriting process was never completed

18. Upon issuance of a conditional receipt to an insurance applicant who has paid the insurer an initial premium

    A. the applicant forfeits his or her right to a permanent contract
    B. the applicant eliminates the need to provide the usual application information
    C. the insurance company is conditionally assuming the risk
    D. the insurance company assumes no risk until the policy is issued

19. The primary distinction between the insurability and approval types of conditional receipts is when the

    A. applicant pays the initial premium
    B. coverage goes into effect
    C. medical exam is given
    D. applicant proves insurable

20. Which of the following statements pertaining to a temporary insurance agreement is correct?

    A. It provides protection against death by accident, but not death from natural causes.
    B. It provides temporary coverage until an application is rejected or the policy is issued.
    C. It provides term insurance protection until the policy is converted to permanent insurance.
    D. Coverage begins when the application is signed and the premium is paid, assuming any required medical exam is scheduled within three days.

21. Louise applied for a $40,000 life insurance policy and paid the initial premium, for which she was given a temporary insurance agreement. All of the following statements pertaining to this situation are correct EXCEPT

    A. if Louise took a required medical exam and died four days later from an accidental fall, her beneficiary would receive $40,000
    B. if Louise died of a heart attack one day after taking the medical exam, the temporary insurance would be payable as a death claim
    C. if Louise died from an accidental fall a few days before her medical exam, her beneficiary would receive $40,000
    D. if Louise died of a heart attack one day before taking the medical exam, the temporary insurance would be payable as a death claim

22. Each application for life insurance requires the signature of

    A. the proposed insured
    B. the policyowner, if different from the insured
    C. the agent
    D. all of the above

23. Upon the issuance of a life insurance policy, an insurable interest must exist between

    A. the applicant and the insured
    B. the applicant and the beneficiary
    C. the insured and the beneficiary
    D. all of the above

24. Which of the following statements pertaining to delivery of a life insurance policy is NOT correct?

    A. From a legal standpoint, a policy may be delivered by mail instead of in person if all necessary conditions have been met.
    B. A company issues a policy (the initial premium has been paid) and sends it to the agent for unconditional delivery to the policyowner. This is an example of constructive delivery.
    C. A company issues a policy (the initial premium has not been paid) and sends it to the agent with instructions not to deliver it unless the applicant is in good health. This is an example of constructive delivery.
    D. A company issues a policy (the initial premium has been paid) and sends it to the agent for unconditional delivery, but the agent postpones delivery. This is an example of constructive delivery.

25. Delivering policies in person gives the agent an opportunity to

    A. solidify the sale
    B. obtain referrals
    C. build the agent-client relationship and prepare clients for future sales
    D. do all of the above

26. Lawrence signed an application for a $100,000 life insurance policy on September 2, and took a required medical exam on September 4. He gave the agent a check for the initial premium and received a conditional receipt at the time of application. The agent delivered the policy to him on October 15. Lawrence's insurance protection actually began on

    A. September 2
    B. September 4
    C. October 15
    D. none of the above dates

27. Susan applied for life insurance on November 1, but did not submit a premium payment with the application. She underwent a physical examination on November 10, which she passed, and the results of that exam were forwarded to the insurance company. The policy was issued by the company on November 15, and the agent delivered the policy to Susan on November 17, at which time she paid the first premium. When did Susan's coverage become effective?

    A. November 1
    B. November 10
    C. November 15
    D. November 17

28. Sandra was first interviewed for life insurance on March 25. She applies for preliminary (interim) term insurance on April 10. The issue date of her principal policy is to be July 1 of the same year. The premium for the principal policy will be based on her age as of

    A. January 1
    B. March 25
    C. April 10
    D. July 1

29. Which of the following statements pertaining to preliminary term insurance is correct?

    A. If an applicant applies for preliminary term insurance on March 1 and the issue date of the principal policy is to be June 1 of the same year, the premium for the principal policy will be based on the applicant's age as of March 1.
    B. The premium for the principal policy will be based on the applicant's age as of the issue date of that policy, not of the preliminary policy.
    C. The purpose of this type of insurance is to provide immediate protection for people who cannot afford to purchase permanent life insurance.
    D. Premiums for preliminary term insurance are based on the applicant's age at the end of the interim period.

30. Employees may be classified for group life insurance by

    A. length of service
    B. duties
    C. type of payroll
    D. all of the above

31. A company has 1,200 eligible employees for its group life insurance program, and the company pays the total premium. How many employees must be insured to initiate the plan?

    A. 600
    B. 900
    C. 1,000
    D. 1,200

32. If a company has 2,000 employees eligible for a noncontributory group life insurance program, how many would be required to participate?

    A. 500
    B. 1,000
    C. 1,500
    D. 2,000

33. All of the following are characteristics of group life insurance EXCEPT

    A. it is usually written without evidence of insurability
    B. minimum participation standards are imposed
    C. each insured in the group receives a policy
    D. the scale of commissions paid on group policies is lower than that on individual policies

34. Which of the following statements with regard to group term life insurance is correct?

    A. Since group term coverage is an employee benefit, employers can select which employees will be covered.
    B. Premiums paid by the employer are tax deductible by the employer and taxable to the employee.
    C. Most group term policies contain a conversion privilege, allowing insureds to convert the coverage to an individual plan if they leave the group.
    D. Group insurance plans must be non-contributory.

35. In writing group insurance, companies use all of the following underwriting guides to guard against adverse risk EXCEPT

    A. medical examinations for prospective insureds who are borderline risks
    B. minimum participation rules
    C. benefits determined by formula
    D. careful group selection

36. All of the following statements about the classification of applicants are correct EXCEPT

    A. a substandard applicant can never be rejected outright by the insurer
    B. applicants who are preferred risks have premium rates that are generally lower than standard rate risks
    C. an individual can be rated as a substandard risk because of a dangerous occupation
    D. a standard applicant fits the insurer's guidelines for policy issue without restrictions

37. An arrangement whereby additional insurance may be purchased at various times without evidence of insurability is known as

    A. free look
    B. constructive delivery
    C. guaranteed issue
    D. loading

Answers & Rationale

1. **D.**   Underwriting is a process by which an insurance company selects, classifies and rates risks. Careful underwriting avoids financial loss for the insurance company.

2. **C.**   Unisex policies offer the same type of coverage for the same premium for men and women. This is a result of unisex legislation which seeks to exclude sex as a factor in premium development.

3. **B.**   All applications for life insurance are not necessarily accompanied by a medical exam; in fact, substantial amounts of life insurance are written by insurers on a nonmedical basis. Part I of the application solicits information about the proposed insured's personal and occupational history. Part II of the application involves the proposed insured's medical history.

4. **A.**   Social Security reports are not sources of insurability information. Inspection reports, the application, the Medical Information Bureau report, credit reports and special questionnaires are all important sources of insurability information.

5. **A.**   The record of an applicant's specific injuries should be recorded in the medical section of the application for life insurance. This is the purpose of the medical section.

6. **B.**   If a medical report is required on an applicant, it must be completed by a paramedic or examining physician called a medical examiner. Medical reports are required when the application for coverage exceeds a certain face amount.

7. **C.**   An applicant's signature is required on the application itself, an aviation questionnaire and authorization form; in other words, forms requiring detailed information from the insured. An agent's report is not given to the applicant and does not require his or her signature.

8. **B.**   Special questionnaires are used to obtain additional information when an extra hazard or risk may be involved (such as skydiving) and to replace the application in unusual cases. A medical report, if required, would be completed by a physician or paramedic, not the agent.

9. **D.**   Angela violated the doctrine of concealment since she failed to disclose pertinent, material information on the application. The test of materiality of a concealed fact is whether the company, had it known the fact, would have been influenced in accepting or rejecting a risk.

10. **B.**   All statements made by an insured on an application are considered to be representations, not warranties.

11. **B.**   The Medical Information Bureau (MIB) is a nonprofit central information agency that was established years ago in Boston by a number of life insurance companies to aid in the underwriting process. Its purpose is to provide medical information regarding applicants for insurance. Private hospitals do not have access to the MIB nor do they support it.

12. **D.**   The Medical Information Bureau (MIB) is a nonprofit central information agency that provides assistance in the underwriting of life insurance. It is not run or accessed by all physicians, nor is data obtained in connection with claims reported to the MIB. Insurance companies report information obtained through underwriting to the MIB.

13. **B.**   To help determine the insurability of applicants, insurance companies normally receive inspection reports on life insurance applicants from national investigative agencies.

14. **D.**   Inspection reports usually are obtained from several knowledgeable sources by insurance companies on applicants who apply for large amounts of life insurance. An applicant's poor credit rating can mean unreliable premium payments, causing the insurance company to lose money.

15. **A.**   With the Fair Credit Reporting Act, applicants must be notified (usually within three days) that the credit report has been requested by the insurer. The insurer must also notify the applicant that he or she can request disclosure of the nature and scope of the investigation.

16.   **A.**   An agent must be very specific when listing an applicant's occupation and duties on the application because of the insurers need to evaluate job hazards that may affect insurability. An applicant whose age is erroneously shown to be younger than his or her actual age will receive a premium quote that is lower than it should be.

17.   **B.**   Provided the applicant qualifies for coverage, he or she is immediately insured at the time of application upon paying an initial premium and receiving a conditional receipt.

18.   **C.**   When the company issues a conditional receipt, it is initiating a conditional contract, which means it is providing early coverage and assuming the risk. The condition upon which the contract is issued is the applicant's qualification for the policy he or she applied for.

19.   **B.**   Keep in mind that a conditional receipt indicates that certain conditions must be met in order for the insurance coverage to go into effect. The approval receipt is more restrictive because coverage is effective only after the policy is approved.

20.   **B.**   A temporary insurance agreement is just that: temporary coverage until an application is rejected or the policy is issued.

21.   **D.**   If a medical exam is required, the temporary insurance agreement would not go into effect until the applicant takes the medical exam.

22.   **D.**   Each application for life insurance requires the signature of the insured, the policyowner (if different from the insured) and the agent.

23.   **A.**   Upon the issuance of a life insurance policy, the applicant must have an insurable interest in the life of the individual to be insured. While an insurable interest must exist at the time of issuance, it need not exist at the time of the insured's death.

24.   **C.**   Policy delivery may be accomplished without physically delivering the policy into the policyowner's possession. For instance, constructive delivery can be accomplished by the company turning over the policy to the insured's agent.

25.   **D.**   Delivering policies in person gives an agent the opportunity to solidify the sale, obtain referrals and build agent-client relationships.

26.   **B.**   When a conditional receipt is used, the insurer is considered to have made an offer of coverage, conditioned upon the applicant's insurability. The insurance becomes effective as of the date of the medical exam, assuming the applicant meets the underwriting criteria and is insurable. The date the policy is actually delivered to the insured is immaterial.

27.   **D.**   In situations where the applicant does not submit a premium with the application, the issuance of the policy (if he or she is found to be insurable) and its delivery to the applicant constitute the contractual offer. The applicant accepts the company's offer when the first premium is paid, and it is on that date that the contract becomes effective.

28.   **D.**   Under the conditions of preliminary term insurance, the premium for the principal policy will be based on the applicant's age as of the issue date of that policy.

29.   **B.**   The premium for the principal policy will be based on the insured's attained age as of the issue date of the principal policy. By using preliminary term insurance, the applicant can be insured without delay and still postpone payment of premium on the principal policy for one or more months for added convenience.

30.   **D.**   Employees may be classified for group life insurance in many ways, such as length of service, duties and type of payroll.

31.   **D.**   If a group life insurance plan is noncontributory, 100 percent of eligible persons must be insured.

32.   **D.**   If a group life insurance plan is noncontributory, 100 percent of eligible persons must be insured.

33.   **C.**   A distinguishing characteristic of group life insurance is its use of a master contract that sets forth the terms and conditions between the insurance company and the policyholder, which is the employer. Those covered by the contract—the employees—do not receive individual

policies and are not parties to the contract. Each insured instead receives a certificate of insurance.

34. **C.**   Employers who provide group term life insurance plans cannot discriminately limit participation nor can they arrange the plans to favor key employees. Any premiums paid by the employer are not considered taxable income to the covered employee, though they are deductible by the employer. Group plans may be contributory or noncontributory.

35. **A.**   Medical examinations for borderline risks are not used in underwriting group insurance to guard against adverse selection.

36. **A.**   A substandard risk is one below the insurer's standard or average risk guidelines. Some substandard applicants are rejected outright; others will be accepted for coverage but with an increase in their policy premium or an exclusion for specified coverage.

37. **C.**   An arrangement whereby additional insurance may be purchased at various times without evidence of insurability is known as guaranteed issue.

III

PRINCIPLES OF HEALTH INSURANCE

11

NATURE OF ACCIDENT AND HEALTH INSURANCE

Types of Losses and Benefits •
Health Insurance Providers •
Self-Insured Plans • *Distinctions*

1. The beneficiary of an accidental death and dismemberment (AD&D) policy receives $25,000 after the insured is killed in an auto accident. The $25,000 death benefit otherwise could be identified as the policy's

   A. primary benefit
   B. principal sum
   C. maximum figure
   D. capital sum

2. The amount paid for the accidental loss of sight or dismemberment under an AD&D policy is known as the policy's

   A. primary sum
   B. dismemberment sum
   C. capital sum
   D. secondary sum

3. Which of the following can be classified as a type of accident and sickness insurance coverage?

   A. Disability income insurance
   B. Medical expense insurance
   C. Dental insurance
   D. All of the above

4. Which of the following statements is(are) correct?

   A. Disability income insurance reimburses the insured for medical care, hospital care and related services for disabled insureds.
   B. Medical expense insurance provides periodic payments to the insured when he or she is unable to work due to sickness or injury.
   C. Both A and B are correct.
   D. Neither A nor B is correct.

5. Which of the following types of health insurance coverage can be written on a group basis?

   A. Disability income
   B. Medical expense
   C. Accidental death and dismemberment
   D. All of the above

6. Which of the following types of health insurance coverage can be written on an individual basis?

   A. Disability income
   B. Medical expense
   C. Accidental death and dismemberment
   D. All of the above

7. Agnes purchases a round-trip travel accident policy at the airport before leaving on a business trip. Her policy would be which type of insurance?

    A. Limited risk
    B. Business overhead expense
    C. Credit accident and health
    D. Industrial health

8. Which of the following types of companies underwrite health insurance?

    A. Life insurance companies
    B. Casualty insurance companies
    C. Mono-line companies
    D. All of the above

9. When available, dental and vision care coverages generally are issued in what type of health insurance policies?

    A. Group
    B. Blanket
    C. Individual
    D. Franchise

10. State-sponsored programs that generally provide nonoccupational disability coverage are known as

    A. income security insurance
    B. statutory disability plans
    C. workers insurance
    D. compensation guaranty programs

11. Medicare is an example of

    A. commercial insurance
    B. casualty insurance
    C. debt insurance
    D. social insurance

12. For group health insurance, employees may be classified in all of the following ways EXCEPT by

    A. type of payroll
    B. duties
    C. length of service
    D. age

13. Which of the following is NOT considered a service provider?

    A. Preferred provider organization
    B. Commercial insurance company
    C. Health maintenance organization
    D. Blue Cross/Blue Shield

14. All of the following statements regarding Blue Cross and Blue Shield are true EXCEPT

    A. they are nonprofit health care membership groups
    B. they are organized on a geographic basis
    C. they are subject to state insurance premium taxes
    D. they offer health-care coverage on both an individual and a group basis

15. Which of the following accurately describes the service approach used by Blue Cross and Blue Shield?

    A. Blue Shield plans provide prepayment coverage for hospital expenses; Blue Cross plans provide prepayment coverage for medical and surgical services.
    B. Both Blue Cross and Blue Shield reimburse their subscribers for covered medical and hospital expenses.
    C. Both A and B are correct.
    D. Neither A nor B is correct.

16. All of the following statements apply to Blue Cross and/or Blue Shield EXCEPT

    A. both are voluntary, nonprofit organizations
    B. under a Blue Cross hospital plan, the insured is billed directly for covered services received in a member hospital
    C. both Blue Cross and Blue Shield have contractual arrangements with hospitals and participating physicians as to rate or fee schedules
    D. Blue Cross plans are designed primarily to provide hospital benefits

17. Which of the following statements pertaining to health maintenance organizations is(are) correct?

  A. An insurance company that markets group health insurance also is known as an HMO.
  B. If a person joins an HMO and undergoes a physical examination, he or she will be billed for the exam and each subsequent medical service as it is performed.
  C. Both A and B are correct.
  D. Neither A nor B is correct.

18. Persons participating in a HMO

  A. pay for health care services as they are incurred
  B. negotiate health care service fees with contracted HMO providers
  C. pay a fixed periodic fee whether or not health care services are used
  D. pay for health care services as they are incurred, at a rate discounted for the HMO

19. Which of the following statements concerning HMOs is correct?

  A. They place special emphasis on preventive health care.
  B. Participants pay a one-time, fixed fee in advance for health-care services.
  C. HMOs generally are owned by life insurance companies.
  D. They primarily provide emergency medical treatment for their members.

20. The type of HMO that employs its own physicians and that requires its members to use these physicians is known as a(n)

  A. closed-panel HMO
  B. open-panel HMO
  C. nonparticipating HMO
  D. general HMO

21. Which of the following statements about preferred provider organizations is(are) correct?

  A. They operate on a fee-for-service rendered basis.
  B. They offer health care services to their members at discounted rates that are negotiated in advance.
  C. Both A and B are correct.
  D. Neither A nor B is correct.

22. Which of the following groups contract with PPOs?

  A. Employers
  B. Insurance companies
  C. Health insurance benefit providers
  D. All of the above

23. Health policies classified as nonoccupational normally provide coverage for

  A. losses due to sickness or accidents that are not work-related
  B. persons in nonhazardous jobs
  C. losses both on and off the job
  D. sickness but not for accidental injuries

24. Workers' compensation covers income loss resulting from

  A. work-related disabilities
  B. any accidental injury
  C. both A and B
  D. neither A nor B

25. Which of the following is(are) examples of health plan administrators?

  A. HMOs
  B. ASOs
  C. TPAs
  D. All of the above

26. All of the following statements regarding multiple-employer trusts are true EXCEPT

    A. they are established to provide group benefits to employers within a specific industry, such as construction
    B. an employer desiring coverage for its employees from a MET must subscribe by becoming a member of the trust
    C. they provide coverage only on a self-funded basis
    D. they are most typically used by smaller employers

27. Which of the following plans use an outside, noninsurance organization to handle the paperwork for a self-insurance plan?

    A. Multiple Employer Trust
    B. Administrative-Services-Only plan
    C. Third-Party Administrator plan
    D. Minimum Premium Plan

28. A group in which a number of employers pool their risks and self-insure is called a

    A. Multiple Employer Trust
    B. Multiple Administrative Plan
    C. Multiple Employer Welfare Arrangement
    D. Combined Risk Plan

29. Distinctions can be made among health carriers in the area(s) of

    A. reimbursement procedures
    B. services provided
    C. contractual arrangements
    D. all of the above

30. Who are the owners of a mutual insurance company?

    A. Stockholders
    B. Directors
    C. Employees
    D. Policyowners

Answers & Rationale

1. **B.**   The death benefit under an AD&D policy is known as the principal sum.

2. **C.**   The benefit paid under an AD&D policy for the accidental loss of sight or for dismemberment is known as the capital sum.

3. **D.**   Disability income, medical expense and dental insurance represent major categories of accident and sickness insurance. Within these categories is a wide range of coverages.

4. **D.**   Neither statement is correct. Disability income insurance pays a periodic benefit to the insured as a supplement to salary when he or she is disabled and unable to work because of sickness or accident. Medical expense insurance reimburses the insured for actual expenses incurred for medical and hospital care and related services.

5. **D.**   Disability income, medical expense and AD&D insurance can all be written on a group basis.

6. **D.**   Disability income, medical expense and AD&D insurance can all be written on an individual basis.

7. **A.**   Limited risk policies are another type of AD&D coverage that provide protection against accidental death or dismemberment only in the event of certain specified accidents, such as a death or injury resulting from an aviation accident during a specified trip.

8. **D.**   Health insurance may be written by a life insurance company, a casualty insurance company, or a monoline firm that specializes in medical expense and disability insurance.

9. **A.**   Dental and vision care coverages are normally found in group health insurance policies. They are seldom written on an individual basis.

10. **B.**   State-sponsored programs that generally provide nonoccupational disability coverage are known as statutory disability programs. They are required in only a few states.

11. **D.**   Medicare is an example of a social insurance program, instituted by the federal government.

12. **D.**   For group insurance, employees may be classified by types of payroll, duties or length of service. There can be no discrimination as to age, sex or race.

13. **B.**   Service providers include HMOs, PPOs and Blue Cross/Blue Shield organizations. They are characterized by providing their members with health care services. In contrast, commercial insurers reimburse their policyholders for health care costs.

14. **C.**   All of the statements are true except C. Blue Cross and Blue Shield plans are organized as nonprofit entities under special state legislation that exempts them from state insurance premium taxes.

15. **D.**   Blue Shield plans provide prepayment coverage for medical and surgical expenses, while Blue Cross plans provide prepayment coverage for hospital expenses. Both Blue Cross and Blue Shield plans operate under the service approach which does not involve reimbursement for covered expenses but rather a guarantee that covered services will be provided without charge to their subscribers.

16. **B.**   Under a Blue Cross Hospital Plan, the insured is billed only for services not covered by the plan. Payments for standard services are made by Blue Cross/Blue Shield directly to the hospital.

17. **D.**   An insurance company may sponsor an HMO or assist an HMO by providing contractual services. Many HMOs are independent. HMO members pay fixed periodic fees whether or not they use the HMO services; they are not subsequently charged for medical services performed.

18. **C.**   Persons participating in an HMO pay a fixed periodic fee in advance for services performed by participating physicians and hospitals. This fee is payable, whether or not the participant uses any health care service.

19. **A.**   HMOs place special emphasis on preventive health care. Subscribers pay a fixed,

periodic fee for the broad range of health care services provided.

20.   **A.**   An HMO that employs its own physicians and requires members to use these physicians is known as a closed-panel HMO. An open-panel HMO, on the other hand, maintains an association of participating physicians, who accept non-HMO patients as well as HMO subscribers. Subscribers choose from among the physicians on the list.

21.   **C.**   The PPO (preferred provider organization) is similar to an HMO, but members pay for services as they are provided at rates which have been discounted in advance for the PPO.

22.   **D.**   While these groups do not mandate that individual members must use the PPO, a reduced benefit is typical if they do not. For instance, members may pay a $100 deductible if they use PPO services and a $500 deductible if they go outside the PPO for health care services.

23.   **A.**   Policies classified as nonoccupational normally provide coverage for losses due to sickness or accidents that are not work-related.

24.   **A.**   Workers compensation covers income loss resulting from work-related disabilities. It does not cover injuries unrelated to a persons employment.

25.   **D.**   Every entity listed is a health plan administrator. HMOs are commercial health

organizations offering health care services to subscribers. ASOs (Administrative Services Only plans) are any groups—including insurance companies—that handle the administration of claims, benefits and other administrative functions for a self-insured group. TPAs (third-party administrators) are those ASOs that are not insurance companies.

26.   **C.**   All of the statements are true, except C. METs can provide benefits on a self-funded basis or they can add benefits through a contract issued by an insurance company. In the latter case, the trust itself, rather than the subscribing employers, is the master contract holder.

27.   **C.**   An outside, noninsurance organization—a third party—that handles the paperwork for a self-insurance plan is called a third-party administrator (TPA).

28.   **C.**   In a MEWA, a number of employers pool their risks and self-insure, rather than obtain coverage from an insurance company.

29.   **D.**   Distinctions can be made among health carriers in the areas of reimbursement procedures, contractual arrangements and services provided.

30.   **D.**   Every policyowner of a mutual insurance company, by virtue of his or her policy, also owns a share of the insurance company. A mutual insurance company has no capital stock and usually issues participating policies.

12

SENIOR HEALTH INSURANCE PLANS

Medicare •

Medicare Supplement Policies •

Long-Term Care

1. Currently, the largest share of the cost of nursing home care for the elderly is paid for by

   A. Medicare and Medicare supplement policies
   B. Medicaid
   C. nursing home residents and their families
   D. medical insurance

2. Which of the following statements regarding Medicare is correct?

   A. Medicare Part B—Supplement Medicare Insurance (SMI)—is voluntary.
   B. Under Medicare Part B, payments for physicians services are unlimited.
   C. Medicare recipients are billed for their Medicare Part A premiums on a semi-annual basis.
   D. Medicare Part A—Hospital Insurance (HI)—carries no deductible.

3. Under Medicare Part A, the participant must pay his or her deductible

   A. annually
   B. once per benefit period
   C. monthly
   D. twice per benefit period

4. Medicare supplement (Medigap) policies are designed to pay

   A. medical costs associated with extended custodial (nursing home) care
   B. most or all of Medicare's deductibles
   C. benefits provided under Medicare Part A
   D. benefits to those who cannot afford Medicare Part B coverage

5. Under Medicare Part B, the participant must

   A. pay 20 percent of covered charges above the deductible
   B. pay a per-benefit deductible
   C. pay 80 percent of covered charges above the deductible
   D. pay a yearly premium

6. Lynn is insured under Medicare Part A and enters the hospital for surgery. Assuming that Lynn has not yet tapped into her lifetime reserve, what is the maximum number of days that Medicare will pay for her hospital bills?

   A. 60
   B. 90
   C. 120
   D. 150

7. What are the sources of funding for Medicare Parts A and B?

   A. Social Security payroll taxes for Part A, and participants' contributions and general revenues for Part B
   B. Participants' contributions for Part A, and Social Security payroll taxes for Part B
   C. Federal tax revenue for Part A, and U.S. Savings Bonds for Part B
   D. State's general revenue funds for Part A, and state's general obligation bonds for Part B

8. Charles signs up for Medicare Part B on March 21 during the open enrollment period. His coverage will become effective

   A. March 21
   B. April 1
   C. June 30
   D. July 1

9. All of the following are excluded from coverage under Medicare EXCEPT

   A. X-rays
   B. eyeglasses
   C. immunizations
   D. foot care

10. To be eligible for Medicare's nursing home benefit, the claimant must first

    A. spend at least three days in a hospital
    B. enter a Medicare-certified skilled nursing facility
    C. have a physician certify that skilled care is required
    D. comply with all of the above

11. Which of the following statements pertaining to Medicare is correct?

    A. Bob is covered under Medicare Part B. He submitted a total of $1,100 of approved medical charges to Medicare after paying the required deductible. Of that total, Bob must pay $880.
    B. Each individual covered by Medicare Part A is allowed one 90-day benefit period per year.
    C. For the first 90 days of hospitalization, Medicare Part A pays 100 percent of all covered services, except for an initial deductible.
    D. Medicare Part A is automatically provided when a qualified individual applies for Social Security benefits.

12. People age 65 or older who enroll in Medicare Part B may also select Medigap coverage during a(n)

    A. open enrollment period
    B. free-look period
    C. grace period
    D. free-enrollment period

13. What is the maximum number of days of skilled nursing facility care for which Medicare will pay benefits?

    A. 25
    B. 60
    C. 75
    D. 100

14. The core policy (Plan A) developed by the NAIC as a standard Medicare supplement policy includes

    A. coverage for Part A copayment amounts
    B. the first three pints of blood each year
    C. the 20 percent Part B coinsurance amounts for Medicare-approved services
    D. all of the above

15. Individuals claiming a need for Medicaid must prove that they cannot pay for their own nursing home care. In addition, the potential recipient must be

   A. at least 70 years old
   B. in need of the type of care that is provided only in a nursing home
   C. both A and B
   D. neither A nor B

16. Which of the following is(are) a common benefit trigger for a long-term care policy?

   A. Prior hospitalization
   B. Cognitive or mental impairment
   C. Both A and B
   D. Neither A nor B

17. Which of the following types of care is described as a broad range of medical, personal and environmental services designed to assist individuals who have lost their ability to remain completely independent in the community?

   A. In-house care
   B. Chronic care
   C. Long-term care
   D. Specified care

18. Skilled nursing care differs from intermediate care in which of the following ways?

   A. Skilled nursing care must be performed by skilled medical professionals whereas intermediate care does not require medical training.
   B. Skilled care must be available 24 hours a day while intermediate care is daily, but not 24-hour, care.
   C. Skilled care is typically given in a nursing home, while intermediate care is usually given at home.
   D. Skilled care encompasses rehabilitation, while intermediate care is for meeting daily personal needs, such as bathing and dressing.

19. All of the following conditions are typically covered in a long-term insurance policy EXCEPT

   A. Alzheimer's disease
   B. senile dementia
   C. alcohol dependency
   D. Parkinson's disease

20. Which of the following statements is true with respect to the lifetime reserve of hospital coverage for Medicare patients?

   A. Tapping into the reserve results in a lower daily copayment.
   B. The reserve does not renew with a new benefit period.
   C. The reserve may be replenished if the patient reenters a hospital after a benefit period ends and pays a new deductible.
   D. If a patient exhausts the reserve, he or she must pay a higher copayment.

21. What benefits does Medicare provide for treatment in a skilled nursing care facility after 100 days?

   A. Coverage for diagnostic services and medical supplies only
   B. Reduced coverage with a higher copayment from the insured
   C. Coverage for physical and occupational therapy only
   D. None

22. The MedicarePlus Choice Program provides Medicare beneficiaries with a choice of services provided by which of the following?

   A. Health maintenance organizations (HMOs)
   B. Preferred provider organizations (PPOs)
   C. Provider-sponsored organizations (PSOs)
   D. All of the above

23. Long-term care coverage may consist of which of the following?

   A. Institutional care
   B. Home-based care
   C. Community care
   D. All of the above

24. The average minimum age at which a person can purchase a long-term care insurance policy is

    A. 40
    B. 50
    C. 65
    D. 70

25. A long-term care insurance policy must contain which of the following provisions?

    A. Guaranteed renewability
    B. Coverage for drug and alcohol dependency
    C. Probationary period of no longer than 180 days
    D. All of the above

Answers & Rationale

1. **C.**   Most of the cost of nursing home care is paid by the nursing home resident out of pocket or is shifted to his or her family. Currently, the average cost of a nursing home stay is more than $40,000 per year—with the average stay being two and a half years.

2. **A.**   Medicare coverage has two distinct parts: Hospital Insurance (Part A) and Medical Insurance (Part B). Medicare Part B is voluntary and may be elected or rejected as the recipient wishes.

3. **B.**   For Medicare Part A, the participant must pay his or her deductible once per benefit period. A benefit period starts when a patient enters the hospital and ends when the patient has been out of the hospital for 60 consecutive days. Once 60 days have passed, any new hospital admission is considered to be the start of a new benefit period. Thus, if a patient reenters a hospital after a benefit period ends, a new deductible is required and the 90-day hospital coverage period is renewed.

4. **B.**   Medicare supplement insurance or Medigap policies are designed to pick up coverage where Medicare leaves off. The purpose of these policies is to supplement Medicare's benefits by paying most, if not all, coinsurance amounts and deductibles and paying for some health care services not covered by Medicare, such as outpatient prescription drugs. They do not cover the cost of extended nursing home care.

5. **A.**   Part B participants are required to pay a monthly premium and are responsible for an annual deductible. After the deductible, Part B will pay 80 percent of covered expenses, subject to Medicare's standards for reasonable charges.

6. **D.**   After an initial deductible, Medicare pays for all covered hospital charges for the first 60 days of hospitalization. The next 30 days are also covered, but the patient will be required to co-pay a certain daily amount. If after these first 90 days the patient is still hospitalized, he or she can tap into a lifetime reserve of an additional 60 days, paying a higher level of daily co-payments. Consequently, a patient who has not yet tapped

into the lifetime reserve days could have up to 150 days of Medicare coverage for one hospital stay.

7. **A.**   Medicare Part A is financed by tax funds provided through the Social Security program. Part B is financed by participants contributions and tax revenues, as it is a voluntary medical insurance program.

8. **D.**   Medicare Part B coverage for those who sign on during the open enrollment period always becomes effective the following July 1.

9. **A.**   Medicare Part B covers X-rays and other diagnostic tests.

10. **D.**   Medicare nursing home benefits are available only if the following three conditions are met: The patient must have been hospitalized for at least three days before entering the nursing home and admittance to the nursing home must be within 30 days of discharge from the hospital; a doctor must certify that skilled nursing is required; and the services must be provided by a Medicare-certified skilled nursing facility.

11. **D.**   Medicare Part A is available when an individual turns 65 and is automatically provided when he or she applies for Social Security benefits. Medicare Part B pays 80 percent of medical expenses after the insured pays the deductible.

12. **A.**   People age 65 or older who enroll in Medicare Part B are afforded a six-month open enrollment for purchasing Medigap insurance coverage. The coverage becomes effective the following July 1.

13. **D.**   Part A covers the costs of care in a skilled nursing facility as long as the patient was first hospitalized for three consecutive days. Medicare will cover treatment in a skilled nursing facility in full for the first 20 days. From the 21st to the 100th day, the patient must pay a daily copayment ($95 per day in 1997). There are no Medicare benefits provided for treatment in a skilled nursing facility beyond 100 days.

14. **D.**   This plan includes coverage for Part A copayment amounts; 365 additional (lifetime) days of Medicare-eligible expenses once the Medicare lifetime reserve days are exhausted; the 20 percent Part B copayment amounts (for Medi-

care-approved services); and the first three pints of blood each year. At a minimum, all Medicare supplement policies must contain these core benefits.

15. **B.**   To qualify for Medicaid nursing home benefits, the recipient must be at least age 65, blind or disabled, a U.S. citizen or permanent resident alien, need the type of care that is provided in a nursing home, and meet certain asset and income tests.

16. **B.**   A benefit trigger is an event or condition that must occur before policy benefits become payable. Under the Health Insurance Portability and Accountability Act of 1996 (HIPAA), the individual must be diagnosed as chronically ill to trigger benefits; prior hospitalization can no longer be used as a trigger. Diagnosis of chronically ill can be based on two conditions: physical or cognitive illness. The physical diagnosis of a chronically ill individual is one who has been certified as being unable to perform at least two activities of daily living (ADLs), which are defined as eating, toileting, transferring (walking), bathing, dressing and continence. A long-term care policy must take into account at least five of these ADLs. An individual would also be considered chronically ill if he or she requires substantial supervision to protect his or her health or safety because of severe cognitive impairment, and the condition was certified within the previous 12 months.

17. **C.**   Long-term care (LTC) refers to care provided for an extended period of time, normally more than 90 days. Depending on the severity of the impairment, assistance may be given at home, at an adult care center or in a nursing home.

18. **B.**   Unlike intermediate care, skilled nursing care is continuous around-the-clock care provided by licensed medical professionals under the direct supervision of a physician. It is usually administered in nursing homes. Intermediate care is provided by registered nurses, licensed practical nurses and nurses' aides under the supervision of a physician. Intermediate care is provided in nursing homes for stable medical conditions that require daily, but not 24-hour, supervision.

19. **C.**   Most LTC insurance policies exclude coverage for drug and alcohol dependency, acts of war, self-inflicted injuries and nonorganic mental conditions. Organic cognitive disorders, such as Alzheimer's disease, senile dementia and Parkinson's disease, are almost always included.

20. **B.**   The lifetime reserve is an additional 60 days of coverage on top of the 90-day benefit period Medicare provides for hospitalization. A patient who is hospitalized for longer than 90 days can tap into the 60-day reserve. This reserve is a one-time benefit; it is not replenished with a new benefit period. Tapping into the reserve will require a higher copayment from the patient. If a patient is hospitalized beyond the 60th lifetime reserve day, thus exhausting the reserve, he or she will be responsible for all hospital charges.

21. **D.**   Medicare does not pay benefits for treatment in a skilled nursing care facility beyond 100 days.

22. **D.**   The Medicare Plus Choice Program, slated for implementation after December 31, 1999, will give Medicare beneficiaries a variety of alternatives from which to obtain Medicare-covered services. Medicare participants will also be able to take advantage of tax-free medical savings accounts (MedicarePlus Choice MSAs) for routine medical bills and a government-funded high-deductible MedicarePlus Choice MSA health plan (MSA plan) for catastrophic expenses. The program will also offer a combination of private fee-for-service health plans and self-funding, and private contracts with doctors for particular services.

23. **D.**   Within each of these three broad levels of long-term care are many types of coverage, any of which may be covered by a long-term care insurance policy. Typical types of coverage are for skilled nursing care, intermediate nursing care, custodial care, home health care, adult day care, respite care and continuing care.

24. **B.**   Many long-term care policies set a minimum age for the purchase of such a policy, with the average limit at 50 years. They also typically set age limits for issuance of a policy, with the average at about 79. Some newer policies can be sold to people as old as age 89.

25. **A.** As a result of the 1996 Health Insurance Portability and Accountability Act, all long-term care policies sold today must be guaranteed renewable. The insurer cannot cancel the policy and must renew coverage each year, as long as the insured pays the premiums.

13

HEALTH INSURANCE POLICY PROVISIONS

Uniform Provisions • Required Provisions •
Optional Provisions • Common Clauses and Riders •
Group Insurance Provisions

1. An insurer may change the wording of a uniform policy provision in its health insurance policies only if the

   A. company's board of directors approves the change
   B. modified provision is not less favorable to the insurer
   C. policyowners agree in writing to the change
   D. modified provision is not less favorable to the insured or beneficiaries

2. Which of the following is(are) normally excluded from an individual health insurance contract?

   A. Types of losses associated with preexisting conditions
   B. Situations involving deliberate acts of the insured, such as self-inflicted injuries
   C. Losses that are covered by Workers Compensation
   D. All of the above

3. All of the following are required provisions for accident and health policies EXCEPT

   A. proof of loss
   B. entire contract and changes
   C. change of beneficiary
   D. misstatement of age

4. Which of the following statements pertaining to health insurance policy provisions is(are) correct?

    A. Clifton asks his agent to make a minor change in his health insurance policy. The agent cannot make the change, but can ask the company to modify the policy in accordance with Clifton's request.
    B. Byron lied about his occupation as a demolition expert when he applied for an accident policy. Four years later, the company discovered the truth when Byron was seriously injured on a wrecking job and submitted a claim. The company could deny the claim and void the policy on the basis of Byron's fraudulent statement about his occupation.
    C. Nellie's kidney condition flares up and she enters the hospital 15 months after her medical expense policy is issued. She submits a claim and the company learns that her kidney condition existed at the time she applied for the policy; she had lied to the agent. Her policy has a two-year limit for a preexisting condition. The insurer can deny the claim and void the policy.
    D. All of the above statements are correct.

5. Children of the insured are eligible for health insurance coverage under a family policy until they attain age 19 or, if they remain in school, age

    A. 20
    B. 21
    C. 22
    D. 23

6. All of the following are required provisions in health insurance policies EXCEPT

    A. notice of claim
    B. grace period
    C. entire contract
    D. change of occupation

7. The entire contract in health insurance includes

    A. the policy itself
    B. endorsements to the policy
    C. papers attached to the policy
    D. all of the above

8. When it is used, the time limit on certain defenses provision in a health insurance policy provides that the policy cannot be contested nor claims denied after two (or three) years EXCEPT for

    A. nonpayment of premiums
    B. mental incompetence of the insured
    C. fraudulent statements in the application
    D. incomplete policy records

9. Which of the following statements pertaining to the grace period and reinstatement provisions in health insurance policies is NOT correct?

    A. Craig's health policy has a grace period of 31 days. He had a premium come due June 15 while he was on vacation. He returned home July 7 and mailed his premium the next day. His policy would have remained in force.
    B. Warren's medical expense policy was reinstated on September 30 and he became ill and entered the hospital on October 5. His hospital expense will not be paid by the insurer.
    C. Under a health policy's reinstatement terms, insured losses from accidental injuries and sicknesses are covered immediately after reinstatement.
    D. States may require grace periods of seven, 10 or 31 days, depending on the mode of premium payment or term of insurance.

10. Which of the following is the usual grace period for a semi-annual premium policy?

    A. 7 days
    B. 20 days
    C. 31 days
    D. 60 days

11. Insured losses are covered immediately after a health policy is reinstated when

   A. the losses result from accidental injuries
   B. all back premiums have been paid
   C. hospitalization is required
   D. claim forms are submitted with proof of loss

12. Which of the following statements pertaining to health insurance policy notice of claims and claims forms provisions is NOT correct?

   A. Charlotte is injured while skiing on January 5. She later wishes to file a policy claim for medical expenses incurred in connection with the injury. Generally, she would be required to submit a notice of claim to the insurance company by February 5 following the accident.
   B. Rex, the insured in a disability income policy, has been totally disabled and receiving benefits for 25 months. The "Notice of Claims" provision in his policy requires that he submit proof of loss every six months.
   C. Gail submits notice of claim to her insurance company after she becomes totally disabled. The company must supply a claims form to her within 15 days.
   D. Furnishing claims forms is the responsibility of the insurance company.

13. Under the required claims forms provision of a health insurance policy, a company must furnish the form to the insured within how many days after receiving a notice of claim?

   A. 10
   B. 15
   C. 21
   D. 30

14. Which of the following statements pertaining to health insurance policy provisions is correct?

   A. Margaret is badly injured in an auto accident and hospitalized for more than three months after undergoing brain surgery. She fails to comply with the 90-day provision in her disability income policy for filing proof of loss. She submits the necessary proof six months after the accident. Because she did not meet the requirements, the company is not liable for the loss.
   B. An insured's time limit for filing proof of loss is 90 days after the insurance company becomes liable for the loss, unless the claimant is not legally responsible, in which case the limit is extended to one year.
   C. Willard submits a claim as required for medical expenses covered by his medical expense policy. Under the time payment of claims provision, the company must pay the claim within 60 days.
   D. Gerald files an accident claim for disability income benefits. According to the time payment of claims provision, his policy could specify paying his disability benefits monthly or quarterly.

15. Under what circumstances can a claim associated with a preexisting condition be denied, assuming the policy's contestable period has expired?

   A. Losses associated with preexisting conditions are permanently excluded; an associated claim would never be paid
   B. In the event the applicant concealed the condition and it was not noted on the application
   C. Losses associated with preexisting conditions are always covered, assuming the contestable period has expired
   D. In the event the condition has been specifically excluded from the policy, by name or description

16. Thomas, an insured, submits a claim and proof of loss for medical expenses covered by his major medical policy. According to the time of payment of claims provision, how soon must the company pay the claim?

    A. Immediately
    B. Within 30 days
    C. Within 90 days
    D. Within 150 days

17. Under the time of payment of claims provision, policies that provide for periodic payment of benefits (such as disability income policies) must pay such benefits at least

    A. quarterly
    B. monthly
    C. bimonthly
    D. semiannually

18. Which of the following statements pertaining to health insurance policy provisions is NOT correct?

    A. The only named beneficiary in an accident policy died before the insured was killed in a car accident. According to the policy's payment of claims provision, the death benefit will be paid to the insured's estate.
    B. Richard, the insured, dies and there is some doubt as to who is legally qualified to receive the $50,000 accidental death benefit. The family is financially hard-pressed to pay some of the insured's final expenses. The policy's payment of claims provision may help solve the family's financial problem by allowing the insurer to pay the family up to $1,000 of the benefits.
    C. The payment of claims provision may give the insured the right to assign medical expense benefits to a hospital or physician in payment for services.
    D. When a death claim is pending, it is necessary for an insurer to have the beneficiary's permission before an autopsy can be performed on the body of the insured.

19. Which of the following statements pertaining to provisions in health insurance policies is correct?

    A. The physical exam and autopsy provision entitles an insurance company, at the insured's expense, to conduct physical examinations of the insured during a claim period.
    B. The change of occupation provision describes the changes the insured must make at his or her job to remain in compliance with the terms of a health or accident policy.
    C. The misstatement of age provision allows the insurer to adjust the benefits payable under the policy if the age of the insured was misstated when the policy was applied for.
    D. The legal action provision prohibits the insurer from taking legal action against the insured in a claim dispute until after 60 days from the time the claim was filed.

20. With what provision of a standard health insurance policy would the following clause be associated?

    "The insured and the insurer shall have the same rights thereunder as they had under the policy immediately before the due date of the defaulted premium."

    A. Grace period provision
    B. Cancellation provision
    C. Reinstatement provision
    D. Time limit on certain defenses provision

21. Hubert, the insured, changes to a more hazardous job than the one he had when he applied for his disability income policy. According to the policy's change of occupation provision, what will happen when the insurer learns of his job change?

    A. A specified percent of benefits penalty will be charged against any future benefit payments.
    B. There is nothing the insurer can do as long as Hubert pays the premiums for the policy.
    C. Policy benefits will be reduced to an amount the premiums would have purchased originally based on the more hazardous occupation.
    D. The insurer will cancel the policy unless Hubert pays an additional premium to cover the higher risk.

22. Under the misstatement of age provision in a health insurance policy, what can a company do if it discovers that an insured gave a wrong age at the time of application?

    A. Cancel the policy
    B. Increase the premium
    C. Adjust the benefits
    D. Assess a penalty

23. According to the optional misstatement of age provision, all of the following statements are true EXCEPT

    A. if the insured actually was younger at the time of application than shown in the policy, benefits would be increased
    B. if the insured actually was older at the time of application than shown in the policy, benefits would be reduced
    C. if the insured actually was older at the time of application than shown in the policy, the excess premiums paid would be refunded
    D. if the age of the insured is misstated at the time of application, all amounts payable under the policy would be what the premiums paid would have purchased at the correct age

24. Which of the following statements pertaining to health insurance policy provisions is NOT correct?

    A. Velma, the insured, changes to a more hazardous job than the one she had when she applied for her accident policy. When she files a claim and the insurer learns of her new job, her benefits will be reduced to the amount her premiums would have purchased had her classification been changed to reflect her more hazardous job.
    B. Ernest, the insured, changes to a less hazardous job after paying a high premium for his accident policy because of his original occupational classification. When he files a claim a few years later and the company learns of his job change, it will pay the full original benefit and refund the excess premiums paid.
    C. If the company learns that Antonio was really younger than shown in his application when he applied for his accident policy, his benefits from his accident policy would remain the same and the company would refund excess premiums paid.
    D. If the company learns that Evangeline was actually older than stated in her application when she applied for her accident policy, her policy benefits will be reduced.

25. The optional provision, other insurance in this insurer, is specifically designed to

    A. limit the risk with any one individual insured by the company
    B. avoid issuing two policies on an insured person
    C. restrict an insured's coverage to one type of accident and health insurance
    D. discount the premiums if more than one policy is issued to insure the same individual

26. How does an insurer treat benefits that are payable for expenses incurred when the company accepted the risk without being notified of other existing coverage for the same risk?

A. It deducts them.
B. It estimates them.
C. It prorates them.
D. It eliminates them.

27. If total disability (loss-of-time) benefits from all disability income coverage for the same loss exceed the insured's monthly earnings at the time of disability, what is the insurer's liability to the insured?

A. The insurer must pay the total benefits as specified in the policy.
B. The insurer can cancel the policy, claiming overinsurance.
C. The insurer must pay the proportionate amount of benefits that the insured's earnings bear to the total benefits.
D. The insurer can reduce the benefits payable by half.

28. Naomi is killed in an auto accident before she is able to pay the semiannual $80 premium on her $30,000 accident policy. Under the policy's unpaid premium provision, her beneficiary will receive a check for

A. $0
B. $29,840
C. $29,920
D. $30,000

29. All of the following specify owner's rights in a health insurance policy EXCEPT

A. unpaid premium provision
B. incontestable provision
C. grace period provision
D. reinstatement provision

30. Under the standard cancellation provision, a company has the right to cancel a policy at any time with how many days written notice to the insured?

A. 5 days
B. 15 days
C. 30 days
D. 60 days

31. Any standard health insurance policy provision that is in conflict with a state statute

A. is automatically amended to conform to the state statute
B. is deleted entirely from the policy
C. is kept in the policy verbatim, but with a rider added
D. supersedes the statue, and remains in force

32. Under the optional illegal occupation provision, which of the following applies if a loss occurs while the insured is participating in a felony or an illegal occupation?

A. The insured's policy is automatically canceled.
B. The insurer is not liable for that specific loss.
C. Benefits are reduced by an amount specified in the policy.
D. The policy is voided, as if it were never issued.

33. The insurer under a health policy is not liable for any loss attributable to the insured being under the influence of

A. alcohol
B. narcotics
C. both A and B
D. neither A nor B

34. A broad statement that generally appears on the first page of a health insurance policy and specifies conditions under which benefits will be paid is known as the

A. assurance clause
B. warranty provision
C. insuring clause
D. guaranty provision

35. All of the following statements are applicable to the insuring clause EXCEPT

A. it identifies the insured and the insurer
B. it defines losses not covered by the policy
C. it usually specifies that the benefits are subject to all provisions and terms stated in the policy
D. it represents the insurers promise to pay benefits for specific kinds of losses

36. Which of the following words relates directly to the consideration clause?

    A. Endorsement
    B. Premium
    C. Exclusion
    D. Beneficiary

37. Concerning the consideration for a health insurance policy, all of the following statements are correct EXCEPT

    A. the consideration clause may specify the insured's right to renew the policy
    B. two principal elements of the consideration clause are the premium payment and the application
    C. the amount and frequency of premium payment are stated in the consideration clause
    D. a consideration clause may be included in a rider, if requested by the insured

38. Generally, the consideration clause

    A. lists the effective date of the contract
    B. defines the initial term of the policy
    C. does both A and B
    D. does neither A nor B

39. After a health insurance policy is in force, the initial period of time that often must pass before a loss due to sickness can be covered is known as the

    A. probationary period
    B. trial term
    C. elimination period
    D. preexisting interval

40. The purpose of the probationary period is to

    A. provide a trial period of coverage for the insured at little cost
    B. limit the insurer's risk related to accidental injuries
    C. give the insured an opportunity to cancel the policy and obtain a refund if not entirely satisfied
    D. help the insurer to avoid paying benefits for losses due to illness contracted before the policy was issued

41. With disability income insurance, an elimination (waiting) period may not apply when the insured is disabled

    A. while at work
    B. by accidental injury
    C. while traveling
    D. by sickness

42. Elimination (waiting) periods in disability income policies are designed to

    A. eliminate claims for long-term disabilities
    B. last generally for one year
    C. help keep premium rates at a profitable level
    D. specify a limited period of time at the start of disability when benefits are not payable

43. Regarding the waiver of premium provision, all of the following statements are true EXCEPT

    A. it is generally available with disability income policies
    B. the waiver may apply retroactively to the original date of disability following a waiting period
    C. such a waiver usually does not apply after the insured reaches age 60 or 65
    D. it is frequently included with both individual and group policies

44. Which of the following statements pertaining to the conversion privilege in group health insurance is(are) correct?

    A. To obtain a conversion policy an insured employee must show evidence of insurability.
    B. An insured employee who resigns or is terminated has up to one year to take out a conversion policy.
    C. Both A and B are correct.
    D. Neither A nor B is correct.

45. All of the following statements pertaining to the conversion privilege in group health insurance policies are correct EXCEPT

    A. some states specify minimum benefits for conversion policies
    B. a conversion privilege applies when a group health policy is terminated
    C. insureds who resign or are terminated have 365 days in which to convert their coverage to individual policies
    D. an insured who is terminated from the plan can obtain a conversion policy without evidence of insurability within a specified period of time

46. Concerning the free-look provision, all of the following statements are true EXCEPT

    A. most states require a free-look provision in health insurance policies
    B. it permits policyholders to return their policies within a specified time and receive full premium refunds
    C. most states require a 30-day free-look provision in health insurance policies
    D. a policyowner need not give any reason for returning a policy in accordance with the provision

47. With an optionally renewable policy, the company reserves the right to

    A. cancel the policy anytime with five days' notice
    B. increase the premium on a policy if benefits paid to an insured exceed a stated amount
    C. modify the coverage if claims filed by the insured exceed an amount specified in the policy
    D. terminate coverage at any policy anniversary date or premium due date

48. Applicants for which of the following types of policies normally would require the most comprehensive underwriting?

    A. Basic medical expense insurance
    B. Industrial health insurance
    C. Limited accident insurance
    D. Guaranteed renewable disability income insurance

49. Which of the following types of health insurance policies prevents the company from changing the premium rate or modifying the coverage in any way?

    A. Optionally renewable
    B. Noncancellable
    C. Guaranteed renewable
    D. Cancelable

50. Which kind of health insurance policy ensures renewability up to a specific age of the insured, although the company reserves the right to change the premium rate on a class basis?

    A. Noncancellable
    B. Guaranteed renewable
    C. Optionally renewable
    D. Cancelable

51. Which section of a health insurance policy specifies the conditions, times and circumstances under which the insured is not covered by the policy?

    A. Coinsurance provision
    B. Coverages
    C. Insuring clause
    D. Exclusions

52. Regarding preexisting conditions, the following statements are true EXCEPT

    A. by most policy definitions, a preexisting condition is one that was contracted by the insured within one year before a policy is issued
    B. medical expense policies frequently exclude benefits for losses due to such conditions
    C. specifying exclusions for preexisting conditions helps an insurer to maintain reasonable premium rates
    D. disability income policies commonly include a probationary period to help control the risk of preexisting conditions

53. Exclusions for preexisting conditions help to avoid

    A. claims for long hospital confinements
    B. more complicated underwriting procedures
    C. adverse selection against a company
    D. insuring persons who are accident prone

54. If an individual health policy is renewable until the insured reaches age 65, when would the policy actually terminate?

    A. The first policy anniversary date which occurs on or before the insured's 65th birthday
    B. The first policy anniversary date which occurs on or after the insured's 65th birthday
    C. The day of the insured's 65th birthday
    D. December 31 of the year in which the insured turns 65 years old

55. Which of the following riders allows an insurer to provide a health insurance policy to an individual for coverage for everything but a certain injury or illness?

    A. Multiple indemnity
    B. Waiver for impairments
    C. Preexisting condition
    D. Optional exclusion

56. An accidental death and dismemberment (AD&D) policy paying twice the principal sum is known as

    A. a reimbursement policy
    B. double indemnity
    C. double consideration
    D. principal twice

57. For group health insurance, employees may be classified in all of the following ways EXCEPT by

    A. type of payroll
    B. duties
    C. length of service
    D. age

58. When an employer establishes a group health insurance plan, what evidence of insurance does each participating employee receive?

    A. Insurance notice
    B. Certificate of insurance
    C. Letter of confirmation
    D. Coverage form

59. Which of the following is(are) a common feature of group major medical insurance?

    A. Double indemnity
    B. Dismemberment benefits
    C. Both A and B
    D. Neither A nor B

Answers & Rationale

1.   **D.**   A company may change the wording of a uniform policy provision in its health insurance policies—once it receives state regulator's permission—only if the provision, as changed, is not less favorable to the insured or beneficiaries.

2.   **D.**   Individual health insurance contracts normally contain certain exclusions and coverage suspensions. These include losses associated with preexisting conditions (to protect the insurer against adverse selection), losses associated with deliberate acts of the insured (such as suicide and self-inflicted injuries), losses associated with excessive risk (such as hazardous occupations may entail) and losses covered by other types of insurance, to prevent duplication of benefits.

3.   **D.**   Misstatement of age is an optional accident and health provision.

4.   **D.**   All the answers should be studied. They provide a good overview of some important restrictions characteristic of accident and health insurance.

5.   **D.**   Children of the insured are eligible for health insurance coverage until they attain the age of 19 or, if they remain in school, age 23. Coverage also ends upon the child's marriage.

6.   **D.**   The change of occupation provision in health insurance is an optional, not required, provision. Nevertheless, many insurers include this provision in their disability income policies because an individual's occupation has a direct bearing on his or her risk profile and one's risk profile directly affects the premium charged.

7.   **D.**   The entire contract in health insurance includes the policy itself, endorsements to the policy and papers attached to the policy. It protects the policyholder by stating that nothing outside of the contract can be considered part of the contract. It also assures the policyholder that no changes will be made to the contract after it has been issued, even if the insurer makes policy changes that affect all policy sales in the future.

8.   **C.**   According to the time limit on certain defenses provision, the policy cannot be con-tested after two (or three) years for preexisting conditions unless the conditions were specifically excluded from the policy. A fraudulent statement on a health insurance application is grounds for contest at any time, unless the policy is guaranteed renewable, in which case it cannot be contested after the two- or three-year period expires.

9.   **C.**   Under a health insurance policy's reinstatement terms, insured losses from sickness will not be covered unless they occur at least 10 days after reinstatement. This is to prevent adverse selection against the insurer. Accidental injuries, however, are covered immediately.

10.   **C.**   Depending on the state, the minimum grace periods that may be specified are typically seven days for policies with weekly premiums (such as industrial policies), 10 days for policies with premiums payable on a monthly basis and 31 days for other policies. (Some states, however, require a standard grace period of 31 days, regardless of the frequency of premium payment or policy term.)

11.   **A.**   Insured losses are covered immediately after a health policy is reinstated when the losses result from accidental injuries. Insured losses from sickness will not be covered unless they occur at least 10 days after reinstatement. This is to prevent adverse selection against the insurer.

12.   **A.**   Generally, a claimant must notify the insurance company within 20 days of an accident under a health insurance policy. Proof of loss must be submitted within 90 days of the loss, but if it is not reasonably possible for the insured to do so, the deadline will be extended to one year. The company must supply its claim forms to the insured within 15 days of notice of a claim.

13.   **B.**   Under the required claims forms provision of a health insurance policy, a company must furnish the form to the insured within 15 days after receiving notice of the claim. Otherwise, the claimant may submit proof of loss in any form that explains the occurrence, the character and extent of loss.

14.   **B.**   After a loss occurs, or after the company becomes liable for periodic payments (such as disability income benefits), the claimant has 90

days in which to submit proof of loss. The claim will not be affected in any way, however, if it is not reasonably possible for the claimant to comply with the 90-day provision. The absolute time limit for submitting proof of loss is one year after the company becomes liable for the loss. Disability payments may be paid no less frequently than monthly.

15. **D.**   A claim associated with a preexisting condition will be covered after the policy's contestable period (usually two or three years) has expired, unless that condition has been specifically excluded from the policy, by name or description.

16. **A.**   According to the time payment of claims provision of a major medical policy, the company must pay the claim immediately.

17. **B.**   The time of payment of claims provision allows for immediate payment of the claim after the insurer receives notification and proof of loss. If the policy provides for periodic payment of benefits (such as disability income policies), they must be paid at least monthly, if not more frequently as the policy may specify.

18. **D.**   Under health insurance policy provisions, when a death claim is pending, the insurer has the right to conduct an autopsy unless it is forbidden by state law.

19. **C.**   Physical exams are conducted at the insurer's expense. The change of occupation provision describes changes that may be made to premium rates or benefits if the insured changes jobs. The legal action provision prevents the insured from taking legal action against the insurer any sooner than 60 days from the date the claim was filed.

20. **C.**   The reinstatement provision provides that when a policy lapses due to nonpayment of premium, but the insured subsequently pays the renewal premium (which the insurer accepts without requiring an application for a new policy), the policy will be reinstated with the same provisions and rights as before (with the exception of coverage for sickness-related losses within the first 10 days after reinstatement).

21. **C.**   According to the policy's change of occupation provision, policy benefits will be reduced to an amount the premiums would have purchased originally based on the more hazardous occupation. Had Hubert changed to a less hazardous occupation (one that calls for a lower premium), the insurer would pay the full benefit for the loss and refund the excess premium to him.

22. **C.**   Under the misstatement of age provision in a health insurance policy, if a company discovers that an insured gave a wrong age at the time of application, it can adjust the benefits. Benefit amounts payable in such cases will be what the premiums paid would have purchased at the correct age.

23. **C.**   According to the optional misstatement of age provision, if the insured was actually older at the time of application than shown in the policy, benefits would be reduced accordingly.

24. **C.**   Under the misstatement of age provision in a health insurance policy, if a company discovers that an insured gave a wrong age at the time of application, it can adjust the benefits. In Antonio's case, the benefits will be adjusted upward.

25. **A.**   The optional provision, other insurance in this insurer, is an overinsurance provision. It is designed to limit the company's risk with any one individual insured. An important consideration in health insurance underwriting is avoiding issuing a policy that provides too high a benefit, which would be a disincentive to return to work. Therefore, this provision sets a limit on the total indemnity for a particular type of coverage.

26. **C.**   Benefits payable for expenses incurred are prorated in cases where the company accepted the risk without being notified of other existing coverage. This limits overinsurance and is known as the "insurance with other insurers" provision.

27. **C.**   If total disability (loss of time) benefits from all disability income coverage for the same loss exceed the insured's monthly earnings at the time of disability, the insurer is liable for that proportionate amount of benefits as the insured's earnings bear to the total benefits. Total indemnities must be the lesser of $200 or total benefits under applicable coverage.

28. **C.**   Under a health insurance policy's unpaid premium provision, any due and unpaid premium (in this case, $80) is deducted from the settlement amount ($30,000). Therefore, Naomi's beneficiary will receive a check for $29,920.

29. **A.**   The unpaid premium provision of a health insurance policy does not pertain to owner's rights. It is designed to protect the rights of the insurer.

30. **A.**   Under the standard cancellation provision, the company has the right to cancel the policy at any time with five days written notice to the insured. This provision is nevertheless prohibited in many states.

31. **A.**   In accordance with state regulation of the insurance industry, any health insurance policy provision that conflicts with state law is automatically amended to conform to the statute.

32. **B.**   Under the optional illegal occupation provision, the insurer is not liable for any loss sustained from the insured's commission of a felony or engagement in an illegal occupation.

33. **C.**   Under a health insurance policy, the insurer is not liable for any loss attributable to the insured being under the influence of intoxicants, drugs or narcotics, unless such drugs were administered on the advice of a physician.

34. **C.**   The insuring clause identifies the insurer and insured, specifies benefits and includes the insurer's promise to pay benefits for specific kinds of losses.

35. **B.**   Losses not covered by the policy would be listed as exclusions.

36. **B.**   The consideration clause describes the amount and frequency of the premium payments.

37. **D.**   The consideration clause is integral to a health insurance policy. As such, it would never be included in a rider.

38. **C.**   The consideration clause frequently lists the effective date of the contract and defines the initial term of the policy. In addition, it may specify the insured's right to renew the policy.

39. **A.**   The probationary period helps the insurer to avoid paying benefits for losses due to illness contracted before the policy was issued.

40. **D.**   The purpose of the probationary period is to help the insurer to avoid paying benefits for losses due to illness contracted before the policy was issued. Thus, many health insurance policies provide that benefits will not be paid due to any illness that commences during the first 30 days (or other specified period) following the issue date of the policy.

41. **B.**   With disability income insurance, an elimination (waiting) period may not apply when the insured is disabled by accidental injury. That is rarely the case with disability from sickness.

42. **D.**   Waiting periods in disability policies specify a limited period of time at the start of disability when benefits are not payable.

43. **D.**   A waiver of premium provision does not apply to group insurance.

44. **D.**   Concerning the conversion privilege in group health insurance, an insured employee who resigns or is terminated has 31 days to take out a conversion policy without having to show evidence of insurability.

45. **C.**   Concerning the conversion privilege in group health insurance, an insured employee who resigns or is terminated has 31 days to take out a conversion policy without having to show evidence of insurability.

46. **C.**   Most health insurance policies contain a 10- or 20-day free-look provision. The common exception is Medicare supplement policies, which are required by state law to allow a 30-day free-look period.

47. **D.**   With an optionally renewable policy, the company reserves the right to terminate coverage at any policy anniversary date or premium due date but may not exercise this right between such dates.

48. **D.**   Applicants for noncancellable and guaranteed renewable disability income insurance would require the most comprehensive underwriting because they allow an insured's

guaranteed renewal of the policy up to a certain age, without evidence of insurability.

49.   **B.**   Noncancellable health insurance policies prevent the company from changing the premium rate or modifying the coverage in any way.

50.   **B.**   Guaranteed renewable health insurance policies ensure renewability up to a specific age of the insured, although the company reserves the right to change the premium rate on a class basis.

51.   **D.**   The exclusions section of a health insurance policy specifies the conditions, times and circumstances under which the insured is not covered by the policy.

52.   **A.**   A preexisting condition is one that first manifested or was treated within a stipulated period before the insured applied for the policy. This period is not necessarily limited to one year.

53.   **C.**   Exclusions for preexisting conditions help to avoid adverse selection against a company by preventing those who are suffering from an existing illness from receiving benefits attributable to that illness.

54.   **B.**   Policy terms are defined in terms of anniversaries, meaning the date of policy issue. If a policy defines its expiration date as the date the insured turns 65 years old, coverage would cease the first policy anniversary that occurs on or after the person's 65th birthday.

55.   **B.**   The waiver of impairments rider allows the insurer to provide a health insurance policy to an individual for coverage for everything but a certain specified injury or illness. This allows an otherwise uninsurable person to receive at least some amount of insurance.

56.   **B.**   An AD&D policy paying twice the principal sum if the insured dies as a result of an accident is known as a double indemnity policy.

57.   **D.**   Group health insurance participants may be classified by type of payroll, duties and length of service, but not by age.

58.   **B.**   When an employer establishes a group health insurance plan, each participating employee receives a certificate of insurance outlining coverage highlights. The employer, as policyowner, receives the master contract.

59.   **D.**   Both the double indemnity and dismemberment provisions apply to accidental death and dismemberment (AD&D) policies, not to group major medical insurance policies.

14

DISABILITY INCOME INSURANCE

Purpose • Benefits • Types of Policies •
Riders • Social Security Disability Benefits •
State Plans

1. Which statement most accurately describes the purpose of disability income insurance?

    A. It reimburses the insured for covered medical and hospital expenses incurred due to a disability.
    B. It supplements disability payments from Social Security if those payments are less than $500 per month.
    C. It replaces a portion of the insured's income if he or she is unable to work due to a disability.
    D. It provides benefits to those who are not eligible for workers compensation coverage.

2. From the insured's perspective, which of the following types of disability coverage would be the least restrictive as to qualifying for benefit payments?

    A. Any occupation
    B. Own occupation
    C. Social Security
    D. Workers' compensation

3. Which of the following statements is(are) true?

    A. Individual disability plans are only available on a short-term basis.
    B. Group disability plans are only available on a long-term basis.
    C. Both A and B are correct.
    D. Neither A nor B is correct.

4. Which of the following is a common exclusion under a disability income contract?

    A. Self-inflicted injuries
    B. Preexisting conditions
    C. Injuries suffered in the commission of a crime
    D. All of the above

5. The amount of the benefit payable under a disability income contract is generally dependent on the applicant's

    A. age
    B. sex
    C. income
    D. all of the above

6. Randy, an employee at a bank, earns $2,800 a month. He owns a disability policy that will pay him $400 a month. Believing he needs additional coverage, Randy applies for another disability policy from a company that has set a 70 percent of salary limit on the amount of disability coverage they will write. What is the monthly benefit that the company will issue on Randy?

    A. $1,960
    B. $1,560
    C. $1,160
    D. $400

7. Disability income benefits for partial disability typically are payable to eligible insureds for a maximum of

    A. one to three months
    B. three to six months
    C. one year
    D. two years

8. All of the following statements pertaining to disability income policies are correct EXCEPT

    A. some policies use an own occupation definition of total disability
    B. in some policies, the (residual) benefit payments are tied directly to the percentage of actual earnings lost
    C. benefits are payable as specified, weekly or monthly
    D. benefits may be payable for disabilities resulting from either accidental injury or sickness, and there are no exclusions

9. Insurance companies control the benefits payable in their disability income policies by

    A. limiting the benefit amounts
    B. including elimination periods
    C. doing both A and B
    D. doing neither A nor B

10. All of the following statements pertaining to recurrent disabilities for disability income insurance are correct EXCEPT

    A. a recurrent disability is one that the insured experiences more than once
    B. a recurrent disability policy provision would have no effect on the payment of benefits
    C. a new elimination period may or may not be required for a recurrent disability
    D. a recurrent disability may begin a new benefit period

11. What is the initial period of time specified in a disability income policy that must pass, after a policy is in force, before a loss due to sickness can be covered?

    A. Preexisting term
    B. Probationary period
    C. Temporary interval
    D. Elimination period

12. Which of the following statements pertaining to disability income insurance is NOT correct?

    A. The probationary period is an initial time specified to elapse after the policy is in force before the insured qualifies for sickness and accident benefits.
    B. Terry is disabled in a car accident that occurs six days after the issue date of his policy. The 15-day probationary period included in his policy would not affect the payment of benefits to him.
    C. Wanda's disability income policy has a two-year benefit period for total disability. She has been involved in an auto accident and now is classified as partially disabled. She can expect to receive benefits for less than two years.
    D. Martin, a sales representative, has disability income insurance that would pay him $1,500 per month for five years should he become totally disabled. If he were to lose a hand in a mowing accident, his policy would not pay benefits for total disability.

13. In disability income insurance, an elimination period is a

   A. period of time when benefits being paid are temporarily discontinued to encourage the insured to return to work
   B. period of days following the start of disability during which benefits are not payable
   C. period of time preceding the benefit period in cases of disabilities caused by an accident rather than illness
   D. 30-day period following the end of a disability before benefits for a recurrent disability would be payable

14. All of the following statements apply to an elimination period EXCEPT

   A. the shorter the elimination period, the lower the premium for comparable disability benefits
   B. elimination periods eliminate claims for short-term disabilities
   C. elimination periods usually range from one week to one year or longer, but most are at least 30 days
   D. depending on the policy, elimination periods may apply only to disabilities caused by sickness and not to disabilities caused by accident

15. Durwood is hospitalized with leukemia and, upon checking his disability income policy, learns that he will not be eligible for benefits for at least 60 days. That would indicate his policy probably has a 60-day

   A. elimination period
   B. probationary period
   C. benefit period
   D. disability period

16. Which of the following terms best describes the maximum length of time that disability income benefits will be paid to the disabled insured?

   A. Coverage period
   B. Benefit period
   C. Disability period
   D. Elimination period

17. Benefit periods for short-term disability income policies typically vary from

   A. one to 12 months
   B. three months to three years
   C. six months to two years
   D. one to five years

18. Sidney makes $3,000 per month as a machine shop supervisor. His disability income policy provides for a monthly payment of $2,500 in the event of total disability. If Sidney were to become partially disabled, but continued to work at 60 percent of his pay, what would the policy pay, assuming it had a residual disability provision?

   A. $2,500 a month
   B. $1,200 a month
   C. $1,000 a month
   D. $0, since Sidney was not fully disabled

19. Which of the following terms relates to disability income insurance?

   A. Service basis
   B. First dollar
   C. Residual basis
   D. Coinsurance

20. What disability policy can be used to fund buy-sell agreements between partners or stockholders in a closely held corporation?

   A. Business overhead expense policy
   B. Disability buy-out policy
   C. Key-person disability policy
   D. All of the above

21. What disability policy indemnifies the business for certain expenses incurred when only the business owner is disabled?

   A. Business overhead expense policy
   B. Disability buy-out policy
   C. Cash value policy
   D. Key-person disability policy

22. All of the following statements pertaining to waiver of premium in health insurance policies are correct EXCEPT

    A. it exempts an insured from paying premiums during periods of permanent and total disability
    B. it may be applied retroactively, after the insured has been disabled for a specified period
    C. it is applicable only to a specified age, such as 60 or 65
    D. it applies to both medical expense and disability income policies

23. Which statement best describes the policy provision for the payment of additional income when the insured is eligible for social insurance benefits but those benefits have not yet begun?

    A. Guaranteed insurability rider
    B. Cost-of-living adjustment rider
    C. Social Security rider
    D. Interim benefit rider

24. Which of the following best describes the purpose of key-person or key-executive disability insurance?

    A. It indemnifies the business to cover expenses and losses incurred when a key person is disabled.
    B. It provides tax-favored disability income benefits to a key person should he or she become disabled.
    C. Both A and B
    D. Neither A nor B

25. A guaranteed insurability rider may be attached to which of the following type(s) of policy?

    A. Disability income
    B. Medical expense
    C. Accidental death and dismemberment
    D. All of the above

26. Which of the following riders provides for changes in the benefit payable based on changes in the Consumer Price Index?

    A. Guaranteed insurability rider
    B. Cost of living adjustment rider
    C. Social Security rider
    D. Payables rider

27. An eligible applicant for Social Security disability benefits must

    A. be under age 65
    B. enjoy a fully insured status under the Social Security program
    C. be unable to engage in gainful work for at least five months prior to the benefit payout
    D. comply with all of the above

28. To qualify for Social Security disability benefits, the disability must be the result of a medically determinable physical or mental impairment that can result in blindness, death or last at least

    A. 12 months
    B. 24 months
    C. 48 months
    D. 60 months or more

29. If a disabled worker who has collected Social Security disability benefits recovers and is then disabled again, must he or she incur another five-month waiting period?

    A. Yes, in every case.
    B. No, in no case.
    C. No, if the second disability occurs within five years.
    D. No, if the second disability occurs after five years.

30. An example of a state-administered disability program is

    A. Medicare
    B. workers' compensation
    C. Medigap
    D. none of the above

31. All of the following statements are true of workers' compensation insurance EXCEPT

    A. benefits are uniform throughout the states
    B. it pertains to work-related injuries or diseases
    C. employees do not contribute to the plan
    D. most laws permit the purchase of commercial workers' compensation insurance

Answers & Rationale

1. **C.** The purpose of disability income insurance is to replace a portion of the insured's earned income when he or she is disabled and unable to work.

2. **B.** From the insured's perspective, qualifying for disability benefits would be at least restrictive under an own occupation policy, which requires that the insured be unable to work at his or her own occupation, because of a disabling sickness or injury, from any cause. Such a policy is more expensive and difficult to qualify for. An any occupation definition requires that the insured be unable to work at any job for which he or she is qualified; Social Security requires that the insured be unable to perform at any gainful employment; and workers' compensation provides benefits only if the individual is disabled because of employment-related injury or illness.

3. **D.** Both individual and group insured disability income plans are available on short-term and long-term bases, meaning how long benefits are payable. Short-term plans generally provide benefits for six months to two years; long-term plans provide benefits longer than two years, often until the insured reaches age 65.

4. **D.** Self-inflicted injuries, preexisting conditions and injuries suffered in the commission of a crime are common exclusions found in disability income insurance contracts.

5. **C.** The amount of disability income protection a company will write on one individual is typically dependent on that person's salary or wages. For example, a person earning $2,000 per month may be limited by Company A to a monthly benefit of 60 percent of income or $1,200.

6. **B.** Since Randy already has $400 per month in coverage, the company will issue no more than $1,560. The benefit from both companies would total $1,960, or 70 percent of Randy's salary.

7. **B.** Disability income benefits for partial disability (an inability to perform one or more important job duties) typically are payable to eligible insureds for a maximum of three to six months.

8. **D.** Disability income policies, like all insurance policies, have coverage exclusions.

9. **C.** Insurance companies control the benefits payable in their disability income policies by limiting the benefit amounts, by including elimination periods and by specifying benefit periods.

10. **B.** Policy provisions dealing with recurrent disabilities determine how and when benefits are payable.

11. **B.** The probationary period is the initial period of time specified in a disability income policy that must pass, after a policy is in force, before a loss due to sickness can be covered. This provision is designed to protect the insurer against adverse selection.

12. **A.** The probationary period in a disability income policy is the initial period of time that must pass before the insured qualifies for benefits due to sickness. The probationary period does not apply to benefits payable due to accidents.

13. **B.** In disability income insurance, an elimination period is a period of days following the start of a disability during which time benefits are not payable. Elimination periods vary between one week and one year; the longer the elimination period, the smaller the premium.

14. **A.** The longer the elimination period, the lower the premium for comparable disability benefits. An elimination period can be compared to a deductible since both are cost-sharing devices that can have a direct bearing on the amount of premium required of the policyowner.

15. **A.** An elimination period is the time following an illness or disability during which benefits are not payable.

16. **B.** The benefit period is the maximum length of time that disability income benefits will be paid to the disabled insured. The longer the benefit period, the higher the cost of the policy.

17. **C.** Benefit periods for short-term disability income policies typically vary from six

months to two years. In contrast, long-term disability policies carry benefit periods of two years and longer.

18.   **C.**   A residual disability income policy ties the benefit payments directly to the proportion of actual earnings lost. In this problem, since Sidney is earning 60 percent of his predisability pay, the residual benefit would be 40 percent of the full benefit, or $1,000 (.40 × $2,500).

19.   **C.**   Disability income insurance contracts may be written on a residual basis, which means that they will provide benefits for loss of earnings without regard for occupational status and even if the insured is able to return to work on a full-time basis. The benefit is payable if the insured's earnings are reduced by a specified percentage below his or her predisability earnings.

20.   **B.**   The disability buy-out policy is used to fund buy-sell agreements between partners or stockholders in a closely held corporation should a partner or stockholder become disabled.

21.   **A.**   The business overhead expense policy indemnifies the business for certain expenses incurred when the business owner is disabled. These expenses, known as overhead, include rents, utilities, and other similar expenses related to the daily operation of the business.

22.   **D.**   The waiver of premium provision applies to disability income policies only.

23.   **C.**   The Social Security rider, sometimes called the social insurance substitute rider, provides for the payment of additional income when the insured is eligible for social insurance benefits but those benefits have not yet begun, have been denied or have begun in an amount less than the benefit amount of the rider.

24.   **A.**   The purpose of key-person disability insurance is to indemnify a business for expenses and losses incurred while a key employee is dis-

abled; it does not benefit the key person. Typically, these expenses are those incurred while finding, hiring and training a replacement for the disabled key employee.

25.   **A.**   The guaranteed insurability rider may be attached only to a disability income policy. To qualify for the option, the insured must experience total disability for longer than a specified period.

26.   **B.**   The cost of living adjustment (COLA) rider allows for indexing the monthly or weekly benefit payable under a disability policy to changes in the Consumer Price Index.

27.   **D.**   An eligible applicant for Social Security disability benefits must be under age 65 (since all benefits paid after age 65 are classified as retirement benefits), enjoy a fully insured status and be unable to engage in gainful work for at least five months before the start of the benefits.

28.   **A.**   Disability under the Social Security program must be the result of medically determinable physical or mental impairment that can result in blindness, death or last at least 12 months.

29.   **C.**   If a disabled worker who has collected Social Security disability benefits recovers and is then disabled again within five years of the preceding disability, no waiting period is required.

30.   **B.**   Workers' compensation is an example of a state-administered disability program. Medicare is a federal social insurance program; Medigap is a type of insurance policy offered by commercial insurers.

31.   **A.**   Workers' compensation pertains to work-related injuries. Employees do not contribute to the plan. Most laws permit the purchase of commercial workers compensation insurance. Workers' compensation benefits vary by state.

15 MEDICAL EXPENSE INSURANCE

Purpose • Indemnity • Reimbursement •
Types of Medical Expense Insurance • Limitations •
Exclusions • Other Policy Types

1. The purpose of medical expense insurance is to

    A. reimburse the insured for expenses incurred for medical care, hospital care and related services
    B. provide periodic payments to an insured who is disabled and unable to work
    C. do both A and B
    D. do neither A nor B

2. Fees for all of the following items typically are covered under a medical expense policy's miscellaneous expense benefit EXCEPT

    A. X-rays
    B. laboratory fees
    C. surgeons' fees
    D. use of the operating room

3. The miscellaneous medical expense benefit in a medical expense policy normally will cover

    A. physicians' bedside visits
    B. the administering of anesthesia
    C. drugs and medicine administered in the hospital
    D. room and board

4. Mark's medical expense policy states that it will pay a flat $75 per day for room and board for each day of hospitalization. The policy pays benefits on which basis?

    A. Indemnity
    B. Reimbursement
    C. Service
    D. Invoice

5. Margie's medical expense policy will pay for actual hospital room-and-board charges up to a stated maximum. Her policy pays benefits on which basis?

    A. Service
    B. Reimbursement
    C. Credit
    D. Indemnity

6. Wilbur's basic medical expense policy limits the miscellaneous expense benefit to 20 times the $90 daily room-and-board benefit. During his recent hospital stay, miscellaneous expenses totaled $2,100. How much of that amount will Wilbur have to pay?

    A. $0
    B. $210
    C. $300
    D. $2,100

7. Arthur incurs total hospital expenses of $8,300. His major medical policy includes a $500 deductible and an 80 percent/20 percent coinsurance feature. Assuming this is the first covered expense he incurs this year, how much will Arthur have to pay toward his hospital bill?

    A. $5,900
    B. $2,160
    C. $2,060
    D. $1,800

8. Major medical policies may include any of the following types of deductibles EXCEPT

    A. integrated
    B. flat
    C. corridor
    D. decreasing

9. When all or part of a deductible is absorbed by a basic medical expense policy, what kind of deductible is it?

    A. Decreasing
    B. Integrated
    C. First-dollar
    D. Corridor

10. The calendar year deductible provision of a major medical policy means

    A. the deductible is applied against each claim during the first calendar year the policy is in effect
    B. all claims submitted during the calendar year are subject to the amount of the deductible
    C. both A and B
    D. neither A nor B

11. When separate deductibles are required for each illness or accident, what kind of deductible is in effect?

    A. Per cause
    B. Flat
    C. Per benefit
    D. Revolving

12. In major medical and comprehensive medical expense policies, a coinsurance provision

    A. helps to satisfy the deductible amount
    B. provides for percentage participation by the insured
    C. has no effect on claims
    D. does not apply until benefit amounts exceed $2,000

13. Major medical policies that pay 100 percent of covered expenses above a specified amount and after the insured's deductible contain what kind of a provision?

    A. Blue sky
    B. Maximum benefit
    C. Umbrella
    D. Stop-loss

14. Comprehensive medical expense insurance covers

    A. hospital room and board
    B. surgical fees
    C. hospital miscellaneous expenses
    D. all of the above

15. Ralph incurs hospital expenses totaling $5,500. His major medical policy has a flat deductible amount of $300 and an 80 percent/20 percent coinsurance feature. Which of the following statements pertaining to this situation is(are) correct?

    A. Ralph would pay the first $300.
    B. His major medical would pay 80 percent of $5,200, or $4,160.
    C. Ralph would also pay the balance of $1,040.
    D. All of the above statements are correct.

16. All of the following medical expenses generally are excluded from coverage under individual medical expense policies EXCEPT

    A. treatment for drug and alcohol abuse
    B. custodial care in a convalescent facility
    C. nursing care in a hospital
    D. nursing care at home

17. Which of the following methods of determining benefits under a surgical expense policy assigns a set of points to surgical procedures?

    A. Surgical schedule
    B. Reasonable and customary costs
    C. Corridor offset
    D. Relative value

18. Benefits paid for customary charges incurred during examination by an ophthalmologist or optometrist are included in

    A. disability income insurance
    B. surgical expense insurance
    C. vision care insurance
    D. basic physicians' expense insurance

19. Which of the following statements regarding blanket health insurance is(are) correct?

    A. Benefits change as the group changes.
    B. Persons insured are named in the policy.
    C. Both A and B are correct.
    D. Neither A nor B is correct.

20. All of the following statements pertaining to dental insurance are correct EXCEPT

    A. dental insurance generally is available in group plans, but seldom in individual policies
    B. a maximum dental benefit usually is specified for a calendar year
    C. dental coverage usually includes a deductible provision, but not a coinsurance feature
    D. benefits normally are payable for most dental work, including cleanings, fillings and extractions

21. What was the impact of the 1985 Consolidated Omnibus Budget Reconciliation Act (COBRA) on group health insurance plans?

    A. It requires any group health plan then in operation to cover all employees, without regard to years of service.
    B. It provides a tax deductibility for the cost of group health insurance coverage.
    C. It allows a group insurance participant to convert his or her coverage to an individual plan in the event of employment termination.
    D. It mandates that group health insurance coverage be extended for terminated employees for up to a specified period of time.

22. Which of the following policies pay a fixed hospital benefit directly to the insured, regardless of the actual hospital expenses incurred?

    A. Basic hospital
    B. Supplementary major medical
    C. Hospital indemnity
    D. Industrial health

23. Which of the following types of plans integrates its coverage with a basic medical expense coverage, providing benefits in excess of those specified in the basic plan?

    A. Supplementary major medical
    B. Comprehensive major medical
    C. Hospital indemnity
    D. Basic umbrella

24. Jane, an attorney, is eligible for medical expense coverage by virtue of her membership in the American Bar Association. She would be issued an individual policy at discounted rates. What kind of coverage is this?

    A. Group medical expense coverage
    B. Franchise medical expense coverage
    C. Blanket health coverage
    D. Industrial health coverage

25. Agnes purchases a round-trip travel accident policy at the airport before leaving on a business trip. Her policy would be which type of insurance?

    A. Limited risk
    B. Business overhead expense
    C. Credit accident and health
    D. Industrial health

26. An actress might insure her legs for $1 million under what type of health policy?

    A. Franchise
    B. Limited risk
    C. All risk
    D. Special risk

27. A federal and state program designed to help needy persons, regardless of age, with medical coverage is called

    A. Medicare
    B. Medicaid
    C. Medigap
    D. workers' compensation

28. A master policy is issued with each of the following forms of insurance EXCEPT

    A. franchise insurance
    B. blanket health insurance
    C. group disability income insurance
    D. group major medical insurance

Answers & Rationale

1. **A.** Medical expense insurance reimburses insureds for expenses incurred for medical and hospital care, as well as related services. In contrast, the purpose of disability income insurance is to provide periodic payments to an insured who cannot work because of a disability.

2. **C.** The miscellaneous expense benefit covers hospital extras, such as X-rays, laboratory fees and use of the operating room. It does not cover a surgeons' fees, which would be covered under a surgical expense policy.

3. **C.** The miscellaneous medical expense benefit in a medical expense policy normally will cover drugs and medicine administered in the hospital and other hospital extras.

4. **A.** Medical expense policies written on an indemnity basis pay a daily benefit for each day of hospitalization, regardless of the actual expenses.

5. **B.** Medical expense policies written on a reimbursement basis pay for actual charges, such as room-and-board, up to a stated maximum.

6. **C.** In this problem, the miscellaneous expense benefit limits payment to 20 times the $90 daily room and board benefit, or $1,800. Since the actual charges were $2,100, the insured must pay $300 ($2,100 – $1,800).

7. **C.** Because this is the first covered expense Arthur has this year, he is responsible for the $500 deductible, and then 20 percent of the remaining costs. His share of the bill is computed as follows: $8,300 – $500 = $7,800; $7,800 × .20 = $1,560; $1,560 + $500 = $2,060.

8. **D.** Major medical deductibles may be integrated, flat or corridor, but not decreasing. Decreasing deductibles are related to life insurance.

9. **B.** All or part of the integrated deductible is absorbed by, or integrated into, the basic medical expense policy; then major medical benefits are payable.

10. **D.** A major medical policy's calendar year deductible means that the deductible amount is applied only once a year and that once it has been met, all claims submitted will be treated for the balance of the year without regard to any deductibles.

11. **A.** If a policy defines causes of loss as each sickness or each injury, separate per-cause deductibles must be satisfied every time a claim is submitted to the insurer.

12. **B.** In major medical and comprehensive medical expense policies, a coinsurance provision provides for percentage participation by the insured. For example, a 75/25 coinsurance provision means the insurance company will cover 75 percent of the allowable medical expenses; the insured pays the remaining 25 percent. Coinsurance provisions apply after any required deductible has been paid.

13. **D.** Some major medical policies contain a stop-loss provision, meaning that the insurer pays 100 percent of covered expenses after the insureds out-of-pocket payments for eligible expenses reach a specified level, such as $1,000 or $2,000. The definition of a stop-loss cap will depend on the policy.

14. **D.** Comprehensive medical expense insurance covers room and board, surgical fees and hospital miscellaneous expenses up to a dollar limit.

15. **D.** Alternatives A, B and C provide a good description of how coinsurance and flat deductibles work. Ralph pays the first $300 as a deductible; his major medical pays 80 percent of the remaining $5,200 amount, or $4,160; and Ralph pays the balance of $1,040.

16. **C.** Individual medical expense policies cover nursing care in a hospital, but usually exclude treatment for drug or alcohol abuse, custodial care in a convalescent home, and nursing care at home.

17. **D.** The relative value approach to determining benefits assigns a number of points to different surgical procedures, relative to the number of points assigned to a maximum procedure, such as a heart bypass. If a heart bypass were assigned,

say, 1,000 points, every other procedures point assignment would be relative to that. For example, an appendectomy might be assigned 200 points; setting a broken finger might be assigned five points. A dollar-per-point conversion factor is then applied to determine dollar benefits.

18. **C.** Vision care coverage, normally found in a group health insurance policy, usually pays for reasonable and customary charges incurred during eye examinations by ophthalmologists and optometrists.

19. **D.** Blanket health insurance covers a changing group of people who are classified as members of the group; they are not named individually. For example, a bus company may take out a blanket policy to cover its passengers. The benefits do not change as members of the group change.

20. **C.** Dental coverage usually features both a deductible and a coinsurance provision.

21. **D.** COBRA, which became law in 1985, requires employers with 20 or more employees to continue group medical expense coverage for terminated workers (as well as their spouses, ex-spouses and dependent children) for up to 18 to 36 months, depending on the event that led to the worker's termination from the group plan. The cost of the continued coverage is borne by the worker, not by the employer.

22. **C.** A hospital indemnity policy pays benefits directly to the insured. These benefits are provided on a daily, weekly or monthly basis, for a specified amount, and are based on the number of days the insured is hospitalized.

23. **A.** A supplementary major medical plan is coordinated with a basic plan, designed to pick up where the basic plan leaves off. It covers expenses not included under a basic plan and provides coverage for expenses that are in excess of the basic plans dollar limits.

24. **B.** A franchise health insurance plan offers health insurance coverages to members of an association or professional society. Individual policies are issued to individual members; the association or society simply sponsors the plan. Premium rates are usually discounted for such plans.

25. **A.** Limited risk policies provide coverage for specific kinds of accidents or illnesses. A traveler who purchases an accident policy at an airport would be covered in the event of an accident during that specific trip. The risk covered is limited to the trip.

26. **D.** Special risk policies cover unusual or extraordinary hazards not covered under ordinary health policies.

27. **B.** Medicaid is a federal and state program designed to help provide needy persons, regardless of age, with medical coverage.

28. **A.** Franchise insurance, although an alternative to group insurance, is not issued under a master policy. Rather, each insured individual is issued an individual policy.

16

HEALTH INSURANCE UNDERWRITING AND PREMIUMS

Risk Factors • Substandard Risks • Individual Underwriting •
Group Underwriting • Premium Factors •
Tax Treatment of Premiums and Benefits

1. Major risk factors in health insurance underwriting include the following EXCEPT

   A. physical condition
   B. lifestyle
   C. marital status
   D. occupation

2. Which of the following would be considered a moral hazard in underwriting a health insurance risk?

   A. Excessive drinking
   B. A serious heart ailment
   C. A hazardous occupation
   D. All of the above

3. Why are premium computations more complex for health insurance than for life insurance?

   A. Morbidity tables are constantly changing.
   B. The average claim is much smaller.
   C. Health insurance involves more than one type of benefit and claims are filed more frequently.
   D. All of the above are valid reasons.

4. Which of the following statements is(are) correct?

   A. Stan, age 27, is a devoted hang-glider. His younger brother Kevin inherited his old equipment and took up the sport. Family history is considered a risk factor in insuring Kevin.
   B. Joyce's mother, Andrea, died 10 years ago of a heart attack, when she was 58. Family history is considered a risk factor in insuring Joyce.
   C. Both A and B are correct.
   D. Neither A nor B is correct.

5. In health insurance underwriting, major risk factors include all of the following EXCEPT

   A. age of the proposed insured
   B. sex of the proposed insured
   C. type of residence of the proposed insured
   D. type of policy requested

6. Which of the following statements pertaining to risk factors is(are) correct?

    A. Kimberly's job requires manual labor in a manufacturing plant. Betsy is an office supervisor who does no manual labor. Kimberly would probably be considered to have a higher disability risk than Betsy.
    B. Christopher, an office manager, would represent a lower disability risk to an insurance company than Ezekiel, a foreman in a farm equipment factory.
    C. Both A and B are correct.
    D. Neither A nor B is correct.

7. A primary consideration as to occupational risk in the underwriting of health insurance is

    A. length of employment
    B. type of employment
    C. past work experience
    D. all of the above

8. Gene, Tom, Barry and Mark are all applicants for health insurance and each has a different occupation. The insurer has classified Gene's occupation as AAA, Tom's as AA, Barry's as B and Mark's as C. Based on this, which applicant poses the least occupational risk to the insurer?

    A. Gene
    B. Tom
    C. Barry
    D. Mark

9. What factor in life insurance is comparable to the morbidity factor in health insurance?

    A. Loading
    B. Mortality
    C. Premium
    D. Interest

10. Kirk applies for a disability income policy. He notes on the application that he drives race cars on weekends as a hobby. Which of the following underwriting techniques could the insurer legally use?

    A. Exclude any losses associated with Kirk's hobby from coverage
    B. Charge Kirk an extra premium and cover any losses associated with his hobby
    C. Refuse to issue a policy
    D. Any of the above

11. Underwriting techniques commonly used by insurers in issuing policies to applicants who do not measure up to a standard rating include the following EXCEPT

    A. attaching an exclusion rider or waiver to a policy
    B. averaging total risks pending
    C. charging an extra premium
    D. limiting the type of policy

12. Which of the following statements concerning group health insurance is(are) correct?

    A. A group health plan can accept or reject specific individuals, based on the risk they pose to the insurer.
    B. The type and amount of coverage available to each member of the group is determined by the insurer.
    C. Both A and B are correct.
    D. Neither A nor B is correct.

13. Individual health insurance policies usually are written on which basis?

    A. Participating
    B. Reserved
    C. Average
    D. Nonparticipating

14. With regard to substandard health insurance risks, which of the following statements is(are) correct?

   A. To provide coverage to substandard risks, insurers are allowed to charge an extra premium; however, they cannot alter benefit periods or waiting periods.
   B. An applicant can be deemed a substandard risk based on physical condition only; no other criteria may be considered.
   C. Because of stringent underwriting requirements, most health insurance applicants are classified as substandard risks.
   D. None of the above are correct statements.

15. Concerning group health insurance plans, which of the following is a correct statement?

   A. Experience-rated premium refunds are guaranteed.
   B. Group health insurance plans generally are nonparticipating.
   C. Plans issued by mutual companies usually provide for dividends.
   D. A group policy that is experience rated does not make premium reductions retroactive.

16. If a group health plan is noncontributory, the employer

   A. pays the entire premium
   B. pays none of the premium
   C. is allowed to select those employees who may participate in the plan
   D. must limit plan enrollment to five or fewer employees

17. With group health insurance, two major factors that influence dividends or experience-rating premium refunds are

   A. reserves and taxes
   B. competition and size of case
   C. expenses and claims costs
   D. type of employer and number of employees

18. What authority establishes the minimum number of persons to be insured under a group health insurance policy?

   A. Federal law
   B. The insurance company
   C. State law
   D. The employer

19. From an insurer's perspective, when a group is organized for some definite purpose other than to obtain group insurance, it is known as a

   A. natural group
   B. specific group
   C. blanket group
   D. contributory group

20. The effect of an impairment rider attached to a health insurance policy is to

   A. increase the premium rate charged
   B. decrease the amount of benefits provided
   C. exclude from coverage losses resulting from specified conditions
   D. do all of the above

21. With individual health insurance, all of the following would factor into the premium rate EXCEPT the

   A. applicant's occupation
   B. insurer's reserves
   C. insurer's interest earnings
   D. insurer's expenses

22. Which of the following statements pertaining to health insurance benefits is(are) correct?

   A. Policyowners who have policies with identical benefits pay the same premiums.
   B. The greater a policy's benefits, the higher the premium.
   C. Both A and B are correct.
   D. Neither A nor B is correct.

23. All of the following statements regarding morbidity are true EXCEPT

    A. morbidity tables are based on large numbers of people
    B. morbidity is a major factor in premium calculations for health insurance
    C. morbidity figures reveal when and for how long an individual will be disabled
    D. morbidity statistics indicate the average number of people at various age levels who are expected to become disabled each year

24. Brent is covered by his employer's group disability plan, which is noncontributory. He was involved in a car accident and was unable to work for six months. During that time, Brent received $9,000 in disability income payments. Based on these facts, which of the following statements is correct?

    A. The disability income payments are not considered taxable income to Brent.
    B. Brent will be able to deduct the amount of premiums associated with his coverage, but will be taxed on the benefit payments.
    C. The disability income payments will be fully taxable to Brent.
    D. The disability benefit payments are deductible by Brent's employer.

25. The purpose of health experience tables is to

    A. indicate a health insurance applicant's chances of incurring a disability or illness, based on his or her past health experience
    B. provide an insurer with a record of all its insureds' medical histories
    C. allow an insurer to estimate the costs of future health claims by providing it with a record of average hospital, surgical and medical costs
    D. provide an insurer with a history of health claims submitted for a given geographical area

26. Which of the following statements regarding the tax treatment of disability premiums is(are) correct?

    A. Premiums paid for personal disability income insurance are deductible by the individual.
    B. Premiums paid by an employer for a group disability plan are considered a taxable benefit to the employee.
    C. Premiums paid by an employer for a group disability plan are deductible by the employer.
    D. All of the above are correct statements.

27. Rick, who has no health insurance, incurred $3,000 in medical expenses this year. Assuming his adjusted gross income was $29,000, how much of those medical expenses can he deduct from his income taxes, if any?

    A. $0
    B. $825
    C. $2,175
    D. $3,000

28. With regard to the tax treatment of medical expenses, which of the following statements is(are) correct?

    A. Personal medical and dental expenses reimbursed by insurance are not deductible.
    B. Unreimbursed medical and dental expenses are deductible by an individual taxpayer to the extent they exceed 15 percent of his or her adjusted gross income.
    C. Benefits received under an individual accident and health plan are taxable income to the recipient.
    D. All of the above are correct statements.

Answers & Rationale

1.   **C.**   The major risk factors in health insurance are physical condition, moral hazards and occupation. Marital status is not a risk factor.

2.   **A.**   Moral hazards are habits or lifestyles of applicants that could pose additional risk for the insurer. These hazards are evaluated carefully when underwriting health insurance policies.

3.   **C.**   Premium computations are more complex for health insurance than for life insurance because the former involves more than one type of benefit and claims are filed more frequently.

4.   **D.**   Family history is considered a health factor insofar as it relates to the health status of the living and the cause of the related deceased's death. Dangerous hobbies (such as hang-gliding) or nonhereditary illnesses (such as heart disease) are risk factors, but not because of family history.

5.   **C.**   Health insurance underwriting addresses the age and sex of the applicant as well as the type of policy requested. The nature of the residence in which the proposed insured lives is irrelevant.

6.   **C.**   A physical injury to a person who performs manual labor will incapacitate him or her longer than a person who does no manual labor. By the same reasoning, the nonmanual laborer (such as an office manager) represents a lower disability risk than a factory worker.

7.   **B.**   There are two major considerations regarding occupational risk when underwriting health insurance: one is the probability of disability; the other is the average severity of disability. Thus, the type of employment one is engaged in—and the classification it is given—is very important.

8.   **A.**   For health insurance underwriting, insurers classify occupations according to the risk they pose. The classes range from AAA, which include professional and office workers (the least hazardous occupations) to AA, A, B and C. Classifications of B or C indicate more hazardous jobs.

9.   **B.**   The morbidity factor—the incidence of disability due to accident or sickness at various ages—is to health insurance what the mortality factor (incidence of death) is to life insurance.

10.   **D.**   An insurer could legally employ any of these techniques when underwriting Kirk's policy. However, it is likely that Kirk would not be denied coverage completely; one of the other options would probably be used.

11.   **B.**   Underwriting techniques used by insurers in issuing policies to substandard risks include charging extra premiums to compensate for the additional risk, limiting coverage by excluding certain risks, and restricting or modifying the policy issued.

12.   **B.**   A group health plan will consider census information about a group in general and as a whole, and then either accept the group or reject it. There is no selection or rejection of individual group members. The insurer determines the type and amount of coverage available to each group member through a schedule or other predetermined formula; neither employer nor employee is involved with this decision. Otherwise, the insurer would likely experience adverse selection.

13.   **D.**   Health insurance, like life insurance, can be issued on a participating or a nonparticipating basis. While most individual health insurance is nonparticipating, most group health insurance is participating, providing for dividend payments or experience-rated premium reductions if the insurer's expenses and claims are less than anticipated.

14.   **D.**   Insurers are entitled to charge an extra premium, alter benefit periods or alter waiting periods in order to issue a policy to a substandard risk. An individual can be deemed a substandard risk based on physical condition, occupation or moral hazards. Only a small percentage of health insurance applicants are classified as substandard risks.

15.   **C.**   Most group insurance plans are participating, meaning that in some form, the group policyholder participates in any better-than-anticipated expense or claims experience. This form may be the payment of dividends (usually through mutual companies) or experience-rating premium

refunds (usually through stock companies). Dividend payments are never guaranteed but they usually apply whether or not the group policy is renewed. Premium refunds are not guaranteed and may be contingent upon policy renewal, but they can be applied retroactively.

16.   **A.**   Noncontributory plans are so classified because the employer pays the entire premium. Covered employees do not contribute to the cost of the plan, although they may pay an extra premium to cover their dependents under the plan. Conversely, a contributory plan is one in which both employer and employee pay a portion of the premium.

17.   **C.**   With group health insurance, two major factors that influence dividends or experience-rating refunds are expenses and claims costs.

18.   **C.**   State law establishes the minimum number of people to be insured under a group health insurance policy.

19.   **A.**   When a group is organized for some definite purpose other than to obtain group insurance, it is called a natural group, such as a company's employees or members of an association. Only natural groups may be insured under a group health plan.

20.   **C.**   An exclusion or impairment rider rules out coverage for losses resulting from specified conditions, such as chronic conditions or physical impairments. By excluding such questionable risks, the insurer is able to issue a policy at standard rates.

21.   **B.**   Health insurance premium factors include interest earnings, expenses, morbidity and for each individual insured, the type of policy being applied for, claims experience, age, sex, occupation and hobbies. Reserves are funds set aside by the insurer for the payment of future claims.

22.   **B.**   With health insurance, the greater the benefits, the higher the premium. Policyowners who have identical policies with identical benefits will not necessarily pay the same premiums, since premiums are determined by a number of factors, such as age, sex and occupation.

23.   **C.**   Morbidity figures in health insurance indicate the average annual number of disabilities or diseases at various ages. They are based on large numbers of people, and do not forecast an individual's incidence or duration of disability. Morbidity is an important premium factor in health insurance.

24.   **C.**   Disability benefits provided by a group insurance plan are fully taxable to the extent that they are paid for by the employer. In this case, since the plan was noncontributory and Brent paid nothing toward the premium, the benefits will be fully taxable to Brent. Had Brent contributed, say, 10 percent of the premium, then 10 percent of the benefits would have been received tax free. Disability benefits are received tax free in proportion to the premium paid.

25.   **C.**   The purpose of health experience tables is to enable insurers to estimate the average amounts of future health insurance claims by providing average costs of hospital, surgical and medical expenses. These tables are adjusted periodically to reflect the most recent experience.

26.   **C.**   Premiums paid by an employer for a group disability or sick-pay plan are deductible by the employer as a reasonable business expense. Premiums paid by an individual for a personal disability plan are not tax deductible; however, premiums paid on an individual's behalf by an employer under a group plan are not considered a taxable benefit.

27.   **B.**   Incurred medical expenses that are not reimbursed by insurance may only be deducted to the extent they exceed 7.5 percent of the insured's adjusted gross income. An individual who has an adjusted gross income of $29,000 would be able to deduct only the amount of unreimbursed medical expenses over $2,175. Rick would be able to deduct $825. This figure is computed as follows: $29,000 \times .075 = $2,175; $3,000 - $2,175 = $825.

28.   **A.**   Medical expenses that are reimbursed by insurance are not tax deductible. Unreimbursed medical and dental expenses are deductible to the extent they exceed 7.5 percent of an individual's adjusted gross income. Benefits received under an individual accident and health plan are not considered taxable income to the recipient.